EVERYTHING IN ITS RIGHT PLACE

EVERYTHING IN ITS RIGHT PLACE

HOW BLOCKCHAIN TECHNOLOGY WILL LEAD TO A MORE TRANSPARENT MUSIC INDUSTRY

GEORGE HOWARD

FIRST EDITION

For permission requests, write to the publisher, addressed "Attention: Permissions Coordinator," via the Website below.

9GiantStepsBooks
Beverly Farms, MA
www.9giantstepsbooks.com

For U.S. trade bookstores and wholesalers order, please contact the publisher via the website above.

Interior layout and design by www.writingnights.org

Cover design by Alicia Pompei

Ordering Information:

Special discounts are available on quantity purchases by corporations, associations, and others. For details, contact the publisher via the website above.

For U.S. trade bookstores and wholesalers order, please contact the publisher via the website above.

Printed in the United States of America

Everything In Its Right Place / George Howard

ISBN 978-0-9993316-0-6

ISBN 978-0-9993316-1-3 (ebook)

CONTENTS

PART III ARTIST INTERVIEWS

PART IV INTERVIEWS WITH VENTURE CAPITALISTS

PART V CONVERSATIONS WITH CEOS, FOUNDERS AND ARTIST MANAGERS

PART VI THINK PIECES II

FOREWORD

As I write this foreword during the dog days of Summer 2017, news has just broken that Soundcloud has been provided an 11th hour life-saving investment. While I'm delighted that Soundcloud, a company that the music fan and Venture Capitalist Fred Wilson rightly calls an "Internet treasure," lives to fight another day to both empower creators and delight music fans, I'm left to think, once again, "It really shouldn't have come to this."

To paraphrase what I wrote in my Forbes column over two years ago, and now compiled within these pages, Soundcloud has done nearly everything right in terms of creating a platform-based business that attracted vast numbers of users, but has struggled in terms of ongoing investment and a profitable exit.

To explain this statement, it's helpful to provide context. In terms of dominant Internet business model growth, the period from roughly 2005 until today can be described as "The Platform Era." Companies such as Youtube, Facebook, Twitter, Instagram, Tumblr, Kickstarter and others have succeeded by creating a user experience that facilitates the ways *consumers* of content can encourage the *creators* of content ("Likes," Comments, etc.) to create more, and, in so doing, converting users who begin as passive viewers to creators.

This virtuous cycle of growth is how platforms achieve Network Effect. That is, the value of these platforms increases (dramatically) based upon the number of people using the platforms. The most successful companies of the last decade achieved their stature by creating Platforms that achieved Network Effect growth, and what they all have in common is a user experience that creates a "conversation" that delights consumers of content while rewarding contributors of content.

Essentially, these platforms understand what the authors of the *The Cluetrain Manifesto* informed us many moons ago: the Internet is the fastest adopted technology since fire because it allowed us to reclaim our voices after a too-long period of being silenced via command-and-control type markets. In short, these companies realized that, again to quote *The Cluetrain*, "markets are conversations," and they created platforms that are essentially *conversation machines.*

In so doing, not only have the users of these platforms been rewarded, but so too have the founders of Facebook, Instagram, Twitter, Tumblr, Youtube, and others.

In the same way, for example, Instagram has created conversations around photos, Soundcloud achieved Network Effect growth via conversations around music. Soundcloud's users—both creators and consumers—have benefited from Soundcloud's platform. As a creator and consumer of content myself it's hard to imagine a world without Soundcloud, and I am certainly not alone in this sentiment. And yet, absent their recent last-minute reprieve, that is precisely the outcome that would have occurred.

Why?

There is only one plausible answer: the dominant content that Soundcloud's users and consumers engage with is music. Music is a content type that people desire to share more than just about any other. What is singing a song if not sharing? What is creating a mixtape but a share-able gesture? Arguably, Napster was the first social network as it allowed people to share their favorite music at scale.

People have *always* shared music. In fact, the entire concept of making music difficult to share—via unwieldy formats and/or DRM—is antithetical to its very essence of being a shareable external manifestation of inner personality traits. Music is information, and information is something humans share to help others better understand them.

--

However, for a variety of legal and business reasons, issues related to the sharing of music online have in many ways defined the challenges of sharing information, generally, on the Internet.

Without going too deep into the details of music copyright, songs at inception have two distinct copyrights: one belongs to the person who creates the melody and lyric of the song; the other belongs to the person or entity who creates the rendition of the work.

For example, Dolly Parton wrote a song called "I Will Always Love You." Unless and until she assigns the copyright to some other party, she is the exclusive copyright holder of the song itself; that is, the melody and lyric. When Dolly Parton's record label creates a rendition of this song—on a CD, vinyl album, cassette, download, stream, etc.—the label is the copyright holder of this rendition. The label does not own or control the copyright to the song itself (Dolly Parton does), but they do control the copyright of this rendition of the song.

Most people know the song "I Will Always Love You" not from Dolly Parton's version, but from Whitney Houston's towering recording of this song. In order for Whitney Houston to record a version of this song and for her label to release it on *The Bodyguard Soundtrack*, a license from Dolly Parton was required. Absent this license, Whitney Houston and her label would be infringing on Dolly Parton's rights. Additionally, as part of the required license for Whitney Houston and her label to reproduce, distribute, and/or publicly perform Dolly Parton's song, "I Will Always Love You," accountings and payments must be rendered by those who are reproducing and distributing the song. The label, of course, has to account, but so too do any streaming services, Youtube, radio stations, venues, restaurants, blogs, etc. Failing to provide accounting and payment results in potential infringement claims.

With the vast number of ways in which Dolly Parton's song might be reproduced, distributed and/or publicly performed the complexities related to accurate payments should be apparent.

However, it gets even more challenging.

Imagine, for instance, if a new artist decided to add fifteen seconds or so of Whitney Houston's version of Dolly Parton's song "I Will Always Love You" as a sample into a track that she created. Technology has made such an occurrence simple to do, and sampling is pervasive. However, sampling someone else's work and then reproducing and distributing a work that includes the sample without the required licenses is *prima facie* copyright infringement.

In today's culture of creation it seems anachronistic and generally counter to the technological dynamic to *not* combine disparate elements into works. That is, technology has only accelerated and simplified the urge to assemble and combine works of expression. Everything from scrawled phrases over pictures of cats, to forks of software code are examples of accretive combinations of existing works.

Such gestures are neither *a priori* right or wrong, but they clearly are hard-wired into human behavior; we build things atop existing ones, and, in so doing, new assembled forms of expression emerge.

Law does indeed lag behind cultural forces. While frustratingly slow to change, laws do tend to ultimately reflect the culture's sentiment. Perhaps our culture's sentiment with respect to reconfiguring works will lead to a change in our laws vis-a-vis derivative works like samples, but, waiting for that to occur is not a strategy.

> *"It is amazing how in the past three years how many more of our clients are asking for transactions in bitcoin proving, perhaps that bitcoin is here to stay. We are even researching, in fact, how to accept them as a payment method. We will feel even better when we know that Gucci is accepting bitcoin as an acceptable form of payment."*

–Ashley Longshore, Co-Founder Artgasm

The tension between a cultural urge to create new works and a set of laws that make such creations almost axiomatically infringing is precisely what led to Soundcloud's travails *and* what charted me on the path that has resulted in this book.

I was intrigued by Bitcoin when it emerged. Dominantly, it struck me as a wonderful thought-experiment related to both a challenging computer science problem *and* the very nature of currency.

As did many others, I read the Satoshi Whitepaper with a great degree of interest, and then watched the space emerge with equal parts delight and skepticism. 2013 was an inflection point for me. As a technologist and an artist, I began to have a nearly visceral instinct not so much related to bitcoin, but rather towards its underlying substrate, the Bitcoin Blockchain. This was not the first time I'd had such instinctive thoughts with respect to the nexus of technology and art. I had had similar ones upon learning to code on a Commodore 64 and determining that my dominant interest was using it to create pixelated art; or, a few years later, when putting two boom boxes face-to-face in order to create a rudimentary "sampler"; or upon discovering the Tascam Porta One; or, later, when running the first CD-only label/first label to have a website; and, again, upon trying Friendster.

For better and worse, my head gravitates towards technologies that have the potential to disintermediate anything that stands between those who create art and those who desire to consume art. It always has.

In this context, the Bitcoin Blockchain now appears to be an obvious feather to, as DA Wallach says, "tickle [my] brain." But, in 2013 it was more of a notion. At this point, there was a vague notion that if there is a technological solution to convert currency into code, and then allow for secure transactions of this code/currency with no intermediaries, why couldn't this same technology be applied to other forms of property that can also be converted into code?

The "property" of interest to me is, of course, "intellectual" in the form of Art. The moment Art is digitized—for instance, in the form of an MP3—this intellectual property becomes a type of code. The same issues and challenges with respect to cryptocurrency thus layer so neatly atop those of the music industry that they are nearly indistinguishable from one another.

> *"Here we are in mid-2017, and looking back to 2014, it's a different world with respect to global interest in Blockchain. Thought leaders in the space can now 'see it', compared to 2014, when I would have to explain what 'block' and 'chain' meant when used together underlying Bit-Coin. In that period, George already understood the potential."*
>
> *-Bill Tai, MaiTai Ventures*

Suddenly, some ideas began to crystallize. Fortunately, due to my Forbes column, I have access to people far smarter than I, and, boy, did I avail myself of them. So much of what drives me to write is the opportunity to not only pull thoughts out of my head and attempt to organize them, but also to present "strawman" theses that are really invitations for people to blow over with logic that is superior to mine.

As a Buddhist, I try to both remove ego and greet new ideas and thoughts with some degree of a naïve mind; one unencumbered by too many of my own "historic" biases. Writing, generally, helps me to stay true to these aspirations; talking to people far smarter than I am drives my naivete home...hard.

The columns and interviews flowed fast and furious. I felt that I and a handful of others had a secret, but it was one that we didn't want to keep. On the contrary, we wanted to shout it from the rooftops. Even as Bitcoin's value rose and fell; even as code exploitations threatened the entire ecosystem; and even as many, many people—to my face and in comments online—accused me of being foolish and ignorant and questioned my motives, on I wrote. More and more people agreed to talk to me. As my editor said during this time, "When there's lots of flak, you know you're over the target."

What began to emerge as the interviews piled up was a pretty concise thesis: The promise of Blockchain Tech as it relates to the music industry is that it could represent a way for rights holders to have an immutable record of their works on a database that is not owned or controlled by any one entity, and these rights could be ascribed with a set of searchable rules that, upon being satisfied, would self-execute. No middlemen necessary.

> *"In December of 2014, I wrote an essay proposing that Bitcoin and other decentralized architectures promised a set of innovations relevant to the music and other media indus-*

tries. Specifically, my proposal was to use blockchain databases and smart contracts to do two things:

1) keep a universal, impartial database of rights and licenses to music and
2) to automate instantaneous processing and routing of royalty payments.

Three years later, I still believe that these are good ideas, and I am heartened that multiple entrepreneurs and other thinkers have expanded upon and are attempting to realize them. The World has continued down a path that I had a privileged view of in 2014 as a result of my role as Spotify's Artist In Residence. Millions of consumers have continued to migrate into paid, legal streaming environments, and the resulting royalties are growing gross music revenues at a pace unseen in decades. The music business at long last is becoming a fun and occasionally lucrative party again.

At least three trends parallel this shift in consumption: 1) music is continuing to become a single global market, in which arbitrary national boundaries are mere vestiges of the prior order 2) the album format is slowly giving way to new release models that are less cyclical and more a la carte and 3) digital music making is driving increased collaboration between creators, leading rights schemas around content to unprecedented levels of complexity. All three of these trends buttress the need for rational, real-time, and universal rights management and payments standards.

But building these solutions is difficult for both technical and social reasons. Most challenging is the need to gain adoption by industry incumbents, namely labels, publishers, and PROs. It is least clear to me whether these intermediaries and financiers have any genuine incentive to innovate, and their financial dominance of the industry hampers the impact of any revolution without them. That has certainly been true of streaming, and I expect it will be of decentralized rights management as well. But the jury is out, and many clever and motivated entrepreneurs are pushing the rock up the hill."

–D.A. Wallach, Recording Artist

It seems so apparent now. It was not a few years ago. The articles compiled in this book really show nothing more than me slowly flattening a learning curve with the help of my co-conspirators.

I'm convinced that the above thesis is correct. I'm also convinced that if the music industry is ever to really grow—rather than experience the churn that I expect may very well happen when we reach the point when all those who will ever be willing/able to pay for a music subscription service will have done so—it will be through the widespread implementation of just such a system.

The fundamental problem of the music industry is that many, many willing participants are essentially walled out from it.

As described above, the licensing requirements for works are extremely challenging and expensive. New entrants are forced to consider the fact that if their product does not easily conform to traditional legal/business constructs, they will either pay exorbitant advances or risk near-certain legal action.

Further, if by some miracle, widespread adoption of a non-conforming product does occur—such as what happened with Soundcloud—the likelihood of a profitable ongoing venture or exit for founders/investors is slim, because of ongoing legal fees and/or lack of appetite from potential acquirers to "buy litigation."

These factors send a chilling effect through the entrepreneurial ecosystem; both founders and investors become highly unlikely to attempt to innovate in the music space faced with these challenges.

Thus, innovation stalls. Verticals that are music-adjacent integrate music cautiously, if at all. Verticals that are music-orthogonal ignore music completely. Both run counter to music's ability to improve virtually any product *and* to grow the music industry ecosystem for artists and other participants.

In fact, this closed dynamic all but guarantees a long, slow death where music simply becomes a loss-leader for Amazon, Apple or Google to lure in customers for their other high-margin products. We're seeing this occur already.

To avoid this fate, this decentralized database of works with machine readable rules must emerge. Call it Blockchain...call it whatever you want, but unless and until some way for creators emerges that provides them with the ability to control how and at what price their works are used in an efficient, scalable, secure, and transparent manner; and unless and until those who desire to build applications and/or integrate music into their products/industries can do so without undue risk or cost (financial or opportunity), there is little-to-no chance that we will ever do anything other than churn and race to the bottom with respect to compensation to artists.

> *"When the interview was conducted, 'Blockchain' was not a widespread term in the world. Few people understood what it was, let alone what it meant. Those who did—including George Howard and the founders of ascribe—were working to spread the word and grow the understanding; as well as improve upon the technology base.*
>
> *Much has happened in the two years since my interview with George. First, the world learned about "blockchain" to the point it's now a buzzword alongside AI, VR, and more. But that's a good thing because the challenge of explaining blockchain is getting addressed on a more global scale. Second, the technology has matured. For example, the team behind ascribe found scalability issues in building on the Bitcoin blockchain, and so designed and built a scalable blockchain database software (BigchainDB) and public net (IPDB). And there are more teams working on blockchain for music around the globe, such as Resonate, Ujo, and Jaak. The protocols for intellectual property have matured for the better as well—in particular via COALA IP proto-*

col is more flexible than past blockchain IP protocols and has bridges to non-blockchain protocols like DDEX."

–Trent McConaghy, Founder of BigchainDB / IPDB / ascribe / Ocean.

In the time between when I began writing the articles that are collected in this book and my sitting here now writing this introduction, Blockchain has gone from something few talked about and even fewer cared about to an almost inescapable presence. A wide range of industries—from financial to supply chain to land title—are now not just talking about blockchains, but are actively utilizing them.

Companies as large as Intel, IBM, Microsoft and others are dedicating tremendous resources to Blockchain tech. Institutions, from governments to academia to non-profit, are in the space. There are myriad bootstrapped and venture backed startups attempting to find the elusive product/market fit around blockchain products. I know this because I work with many of them.

It would be disingenuous to say that the music industry is right there with the above-listed players. Certainly, there are no shortage of people who believe, as I do, that the music industry should and must embrace this technology. But, as it so often does, the traditional music industry views Blockchain Technology in the same way it has viewed most other technological innovations — from the piano roll all the way through to peer-to-peer file sharing—as an existential threat. The dominant players, while occasionally playing lip-service to this technology, have not embraced

Blockchain tech in any meaningful ways.

Perhaps, as is often the case, just before industries are disrupted—in the Clayton Christensen *Innovator's Dilemma* sense of the word—this current point in time is the moment when the incumbents still believe that Blockchain technology is not a threat (or opportunity), and go about their business assuming that their moat is wide and deep enough to inure them...until it isn't.

There are certainly those working in the Blockchain space who believe they have solutions that could, if not topple the incumbents, at least provide a very compelling alternative to them.

--

Contrary to the rep on the "street" about me, I'm not interested in toppling industries. My interest is what it always has been: to help artists create sustainable careers on their own terms.

I believe deeply that the way to accomplish this is to facilitate an increasing amount of direct-to-creator licenses between an increasing amount of new entrants into the music system. I believe deeply that Blockchain Technology can power this. I am indifferent to whether or not this leads to extinction or opportunity for incumbents.

I am *not* indifferent, but rather, passionate in my hope that some of the pieces compiled in this book inspire those who believe, as I do, that art is an empathy machine to leverage Blockchain (or any other technologies) in a manner that results in more artists not simply sustaining, but thriving on their own terms.

George Howard
Beverly Farms, MA
August 2017

ACKNOWLEDGEMENTS

This really isn't my book. There would be very little here if not for the participation of those who gave their time and knowledge, and who not only allowed me to talk with them, but also then worked with me to shape these conversations into pieces that—one hopes—take this complex subject and make it understandable. All we really have in this world is time, and so to each and every person who gifted me some of theirs, I am beyond grateful... I am honored.

Speaking of time, my children, Annabelle, and Henry—all gave me the gift of patience and understanding when I took time away from them for what has become this book. Thank you.

To my editors at Forbes, where these articles originally appeared, thank you for not only defying what the great author and songwriter, Kinky Friedman, says is the role of editors, "Taking great work and making it good," but actually doing the inverse: making my work much better because of your thoughtful expertise.

To my colleagues at GHStrategic and 9GiantSteps Books, thank you for driving, inspiring, and supporting me. In particular, thank you to Jennifer Howe for pushing me to make this idea a reality. Additionally, in no way would this book have come together without the amazing work of Alec D'Alelio, Nicole Pompei, and

Lindsay Sack. Each of you is exceptional, and—in many ways—this book is finished because of you. I didn't want to let you and your good work down by not pulling it all together.

To my students, while I hope some of the information in this book will clarify my insane in-class meandering, I mainly want to thank you for teaching me more than I ever will be able to teach you.

Last, I suppose if I know anything about life and how to live it (I don't), it's that if you're very, very lucky you figure out some kind of purpose or meaning that gets you out of bed. For me, that purpose is trying to help Artists create sustainable careers on their own terms, because I believe with all my heart that art is an empathy machine and, thus, more art equals less war. So, maybe this new technology will help get us there, and maybe some of the pieces compiled in the book will provide some guidance. And so, as always, to the Artists of the world, my work is for you.

PART I

THINK PIECES I

The Bitcoin Blockchain Just Might Save The Music Industry...If Only We Could Understand It

Bitcoin Can't Save The Music Industry Because the Music Industry Will Resist Transparency

Bitcoin Is to The Blockchain As Porn Was to The Internet

Could Blockchain Save SoundCloud And Investment in The Future of The Music Industry?

Blockchain Technology Is Our Chance to Rebuild the Internet in A Way That Benefits Creators

THE BITCOIN BLOCKCHAIN JUST MIGHT SAVE THE MUSIC INDUSTRY...IF ONLY WE COULD UNDERSTAND IT

May 17, 2015

The Bitcoin Blockchain just might save the music industry, but first we have to take the time to understand it. Admittedly, Bitcoin, generally, and the Blockchain, specifically, are not easily understood at first glance. However, the implications of the Bitcoin Blockchain not only for currency, but for intellectual property are too great not to expend the time and effort needed to see its applicability.

The alternative is to let the technology go the way of Creative Commons; another tool with tremendous application, but equally tremendous misunderstanding—and thus under-utilization.

Via my work in the visual art world with Artgasm, the company the brilliant artist Ashley Longshore and I recently started, I'm immersing myself in visual IP.

This led me to a company called ascribe. ascribe utilizes the Bitcoin Blockchain to, in their own words, "enable you to share your digital creations without worrying about losing ownership rights."

I'm genuinely excited about Bitcoin. Dominantly, this excitement comes from the fact that confirmed transactions using Bitcoin are included in the Blockchain. The Blockchain is a record of all transactions.

This has tremendous application for IP. ascribe is focused on visual elements; however, the utility of this approach extends way beyond visual IP. Music, for instance, seems to me a prime candidate for this type of use-case.

Certainly, such a process would allow for the better tracking of usage of music, which would lead to more accurate compensation for rights holders.

For example, if I am a performer signed to a label, I could assign the rights to my Sound Recordings, and monitor—via the Blockchain—the ways in which the label exploits this Sound Recording (sales, licenses, streams, etc.). This would *greatly* reduce controversy (and related transaction costs—audit time/money) around royalty payments, etc. Similarly, the label/publisher (or—as I would encourage—artist) who releases the work could lend (i.e. license) the Sound Recording and underlying Composition to streaming services, broadcasters, etc., and monitor—via the Blockchain—the ways in which these rights (Sound Recording/Composition) are used.

In this manner, a great deal of transparency would emerge. With increased transparency comes increased speed and desire for deals/transactions.

Certainly, if the music industry has any hope of taking advantage of the new opportunities available to them via the transformation of music to information it will require this type of transparency that will lead to more accurate information, and thus better decision making with respect to deals.

My fear is that the Blockchain (and innovative companies like ascribe) will struggle to gain the understanding required to achieve widespread usage. In short, my fear is that the same fate will befall Blockchain (for artists) as seems to have befallen Creative Commons; people *just do not understand it,* and CC does a bad job of explaining it (which is a shame), and thus most don't utilize it.

This is really as much an educational (or marketing/branding) issue as it is a technological one. The stakes are too high not to at least try to create the same transparency around the understanding of the technology—even as the technology itself attempts to create transparency around its usage.

Artists—visual, musical, or otherwise—really must educate themselves about these emerging technologies, or suffer the fate of being exploited by those who do.

BITCOIN CAN'T SAVE THE MUSIC INDUSTRY BECAUSE THE MUSIC INDUSTRY WILL RESIST TRANSPARENCY

May 22, 2015

Here's a straw man that I believe fairly strongly: Bitcoin can't save the music industry because the music industry will resist the transparency it might bring. The previous article discussed how Bitcoin could potentially prove to be an effective tool for tracking the rights and transactions surrounding musical intellectual property. However, in my quixotic rush towards some form of musical utopia in which every transaction can be tracked and the appropriate rights holders compensated, I lost track of the very thing that nearly always frustrates this type of progress.

Fortunately for me, an astute reader pointed out this omission via Twitter:

I've spoken to the author of this tweet, Aston Motes—the first hire at Dropbox and now an advisor to many music-related startups and entrepreneur in the music space—a few times over the years, and was unsurprised, given his experience and background, that he made such a spot-on comment.

His comment tracks directly with something I've talked and written about over the years. Bluntly: the parties who benefit most from the lack of transparency are the ones who will resist anything that *ends* the lack of transparency.

Of course, the parties who benefit the most from lack of transparency in the music industry are the labels, publishers, and streaming services. The record industry was built upon a firmament of information asymmetry – that is, **the labels & publishers have more knowledge than those signing the contracts. Given this, they are able to exploit this information imbalance to their benefit.** At the extreme end, this meant blatantly lying to artists who were under-educated, under-represented, under-experienced (or all of the above) to strip them—often, forever—of their rights. At a slightly more benign level, these labels and others create agreements and "reporting" so byzantine in nature that only the most experienced (and expensive) lawyers can parse them, which forces many artists who don't have the resources for such representation to accept the deals/reports *prima facie.*

Yesterday I Skyped with Mr. Motes, and he elaborated on his tweet, "Even indie labels – it's not clear that they'd be willing to disclose who makes what, and what people sell. The whole industry is driven on smoke and mirrors."

He continued down a path that I've been harping on for what seems like forever: the idea that these services could provide more than just economic value – but he tied this to Crypto Currency.

"Why doesn't Spotify give fans or artists more access to the raw numbers, etc.?" Mr. Motes questioned before adding, "Cryptocurrencies could play a role here because they're decentralized, but even centralized companies like Spotify could show more; they could expose actual plays by user, or disclose to artists what songs were listened to, or be transparent about how much money is going to the artist. All of this is interesting information that the majors or any label don't want out there."

Mr. Motes added: "from a technology perspective nothing is stopping [labels or streaming services] from building these types of transparent reports. The streaming services fear the same things the record labels fear: If you let people know how complicated these deals are and how the money is split up it compromises the nice shiny facade Spotify has put up. Showing what's behind this will make them look bad."

If you doubt that labels or publishers have benefited from a lack of transparency, it's instructive to look at how the fast-growing publishing company Kobalt distinguishes themselves from the other, more established/older publishers. The first lines of their About page state:

"We create technology solutions for a more transparent, efficient and empowering future for rights owners, where artists, songwriters, publishers and labels can trust they will be paid fairly and accurately, regardless of how complex the digital world becomes."

If Kobalt has been able to gain market traction based on the competitive advantage of transparency, what does that say about the industry at large?

Certainly, the artists are not blameless in not demanding less obtuse agreements/reporting, but they simply don't have the leverage to do so, and – being artists – their impulse to create/the potential for their creations to be heard will outweigh virtually any other consideration.

Therefore, while my thoughts with respect to Bitcoin providing transparency may or may not be accurate (I stand by the fact that it could greatly help, but absent better education holds little chance), **there is little to no incentive for those who benefit from lack of transparency to adopt Bitcoin or any other technology that would force them to make less advantageous deals, or render more accurate reporting that would negatively impact their bottom line.**

So where does this leave us?

Eventually, the incumbents will face the same fates that befall all companies who myopically focus on their existing customers/business models while blithely ignoring the changing needs of the market – essentially, they face *The Innovator's Dilemma*. Perhaps the disruption will come from new models that, as Mr. Motes suggests, charge varying amounts for people with different consumption patterns, which would increase the number of frequent micro-transactions.

However, Mr. Motes noted that while crypto-currencies could play a large role in this scenario, Bitcoin will likely not be the Cryptocurrency utilized. According to Mr. Motes Bitcoin doesn't have the transaction speed to handle the number of transactions necessary to keep track of the rights. This limitation is echoed by Mike Hearn, formerly of Google and a Bitcoin Core developer, who states that Bitcoin is limited to about 7 transactions per second.

What both of these issues—Bitcoin's limitations around transaction numbers and the labels' resistance towards a system with increased transparency—really imply is that we're on the cusp of change.

That is, rather than there being a vague underlying elusive undiagnosable ailment that is plaguing the industry, we're moving towards identifying the root causes of the issues, which often can lead to a cure.

BITCOIN IS TO THE BLOCKCHAIN AS PORN WAS TO THE INTERNET

Aug 5, 2015

Since I've delved into Blockchain and the Arts with my various posts on the subject, one thing that has become resoundingly clear is that there's *tremendous* misunderstanding about fundamental concepts.

An example: I was speaking to someone the other day, and I mentioned that I had been writing about Blockchain. The person asked, "What's Blockchain?"

Drawing from my favorite explanation, I said, "The Blockchain is a decentralized and distributed database that sequentially records transactions..." I saw his eyes glazing over, and so I pulled my trump card – something I knew would grab his attention—and mentioned Bitcoin.

The person stopped me mid-sentence, and with a tremendous amount of authority in his voice declared: "Oh, Bitcoin is a scam!" With a degree of self-restraint that is unusual for me, I managed to not say what I was thinking—"So… you *don't know what the Blockchain is*, but you're a Bitcoin *expert*?"—and just redirected the conversation.

Often, when it comes to emergent technologies, everyone is an "expert." This is because while the foundational knowledge is being constructed, it is not yet able to be validated by many real-world applications. Simply put, there aren't enough case studies.

Blockchain is currently in this place. There are few show-rather-than-tell use cases to explain the Blockchain. Thus, when people like myself try to do so we turn to future applications; such as, Venture Capitalist, Andy Weissman's "Nirvana State," or Imogen Heap's "Mycelia Project."

Beyond these types of forward-looking examples, the current example that people *do* have some awareness of, for better or worse, is Bitcoin. In this way, Bitcoin and Blockchain have been linked, and many people view the two as synonymous. They are not.

Bitcoin is simply a currency that utilizes the Blockchain as a decentralized registry of transactions.

The problem is that many people—basing their assumptions upon reports of scams and it being utilized for nefarious activities—view Bitcoin with skepticism. My observation is that this has led to a conflation of Bitcoin with Blockchain, and thus Blockchain getting a bad rap by association.

I was discussing this with PledgeMusic founder and crypto enthusiast, Benji Rogers, and our conversation resulted in us trying to better contextualize the relationship between Bitcoin and Blockchain in order to show that, far from being the only use of the Blockchain, Bitcoin is really just the first instance of a technology utilizing the Blockchain that has gained the public's attention.

The analogy I came up with is: "Bitcoin is to the Blockchain as Porn was to the Internet."

Pornography is credited for being the driving force behind any number of technological advances. In *The Erotic Engine: How Pornography Has Powered Mass Communication, from Gutenberg to Google*, Patchen Barss enumerates numerous technologies that were advanced by porn – from the VCR, to e-commerce, to webcams and others.

With its seductive allure of easy money, and its ability to be used for all sort of nefarious transactions, Bitcoin has captured the attention of those interested in such things, and technologies and markets have been developed to facilitate these (and other, less "sexy"...insurance?!) transactions.

Thus, in the same way pornography drove the early development of the Internet, these early adopters of Bitcoin – motivated by the promise of utilizing the nascent technology to satisfy their very specific needs – may end up creating markets and technologies that ultimately lay the foundation for more generalized uses.

Of course, it remains to be seen if either Bitcoin or the Blockchain will prove to be durable solutions for anyone other than early adopters. However, if history is any indication—as Bitcoin markets and technologies continue to be developed—the Blockchain will become more understood, and vast numbers of new usages will emerge. In this manner, Bitcoin may truly do for the Blockchain what porn did for the Internet.

COULD BLOCKCHAIN SAVE SOUNDCLOUD AND INVESTMENT IN THE FUTURE OF THE MUSIC INDUSTRY?

Jul 30, 2015

SoundCloud has done everything right. Everything. It created a bottoms-up, platform-based tool with an exceedingly high viral coefficient and a delightful UX. Utilizing precisely the same thesis that Instagram has utilized for photos, and Twitter has for short messages, SoundCloud has revolutionized and democratized the sharing of audio. In so doing, SoundCloud has attracted massive amounts of customers, and retained them by proving its utility over and over. It's done everything right.

So…why then have Twitter, Instagram, Tumblr, Facebook, Reddit and others—each with the same bottoms-up, User Generated Content, platform-based approach as SoundCloud—all enjoyed massive liquidity events while, according to scuttlebutt, SoundCloud is having trouble raising additional capital, and resorting to things like (gasp) paid membership models?

The answer to this question is not only bad for SoundCloud, but bad for innovation and investment in the music space, generally.

Here's why. The difference between SoundCloud and the above-mentioned companies, of course, is the type of "C" that the (U)sers are (G)enerating on SoundCloud: Music.

I believe we're at the eve of a massive change in terms of what users will and won't contribute, but, for now, most people are plenty happy to contribute their photos to help Instagram attract and retain users. Similarly (with the exception of, apparently, comedians), people (myself included) are happy to contribute their pithy updates to help Twitter attract and retain users. Musicians too, have happily contributed music to help SoundCloud attract and retain users.

But copyright, as it applies to music, is—ostensibly—more complicated, or, at least more litigated, than it is for tweets and photos.

For instance, when a SoundCloud user creates a song that also contains elements of someone else's song—a mashup or a remix, for example—they have created what in *copyright-ese* is known as a "derivative work." Absent a license from the copyright holders of the works that have been remixed/sampled, the user is infringing on the exclusive rights of the authors of the other works to create derivatives, as well as to distribute, reproduce, publicly perform, and, because of SoundCloud's slick visual waveform, even to display.

These types of works are very prevalent on SoundCloud.

SoundCloud, like all other websites that trade in UGC, enjoy certain protections established under legislative acts, like the Online Copyright Infringement Liability Limitation Act (OCILLA), which is commonly referred to as the "Safe Harbor Provision of the Digital Millennium Copyright Act (DMCA)." In short, this Act offers UGC sites some protection from liability related to infringement claims so long as they:

(1) have a policy to address and remove infringing material expeditiously upon sufficient notification, and
(2) do not interfere with copyright owners' technical attempts to protect or identify their copyrighted works.

In practice, what this means is that UGC sites that dominantly rely on music as their content type are terrified of violating one of the prongs above (mostly the first) and thus losing their Safe Harbor protection, and being hit by a mass of infringement lawsuits. This fear leads these sites to *aggressively* comply with takedown notices…whether or not those issuing the takedown notice have any basis.

Even those who rigidly comply to the prongs above are not immune to the high transaction costs related to the systems to identify infringing works, nor from dealing with the never-ending stream of notices—valid or otherwise.

The impact of this combination of fear of litigation and the related steep transaction costs of attempting to stay in compliance with the DMCA has, I believe, led to a chilling effect with respect to ongoing or new investment in music-related startups.

Investors are reasonably determining that there is simply too much risk/uncertainty (a distinction without a difference) associated with the music space, and therefore are allocating their funds to other categories.

This explains the difficulty (if true) SoundCloud is having with respect to finding ongoing investment, and also SoundCloud's inability to find a purchaser. Perhaps YouTube really was the last of the UGC companies able to be acquired, even when, in so doing, the acquiring company (Google) ended up purchasing massive litigation. Much of this "purchased litigation" was, of course, due to the music-related UGC on YouTube.

Frustratingly, this would also offer a reasonable explanation as to the overall lack of innovation in the music space.

Viewed in this way, the incumbent major labels and publishers can be seen to have effectively stifled investment in emerging, innovative music companies via the threat of litigation.

In this scenario, everyone—SoundCloud, artists, entrepreneurs, investors, customers—loses. Everyone, that is, except for the incumbents, who will always resist any change that might threaten their dominance. Even change that ultimately could save them.

One thing that might lead to a breakthrough not only for SoundCloud, but for innovation in the music space generally, is the Blockchain.

Had SoundCloud been able to avail themselves of the Blockchain, they could have become the *de facto* "front end" of the Blockchain, by allowing artists to register their works and create rules around these works for how they could be utilized. Both Andy Weissman and Imogen Heap envision such an approach in their recent discussions with me.

By following this type of approach, SoundCloud would have been able to—at minimum—avoid/reduce many of the expensive and time-consuming transaction costs related to determining the validity of claims/rights, etc.

It's not too late, of course. SoundCloud *could* institute a Skunkworks project with even a small percentage of their artists, and develop a Blockchain-related part of their business to address their current issues, and pave a way forward that would obviate many of their current issues.

Of course, so too could a new company. The problem is that a new entrant would lack the sheer number of potential participants, not to mention the brand equity, that SoundCloud has. Thus, it would be a much slower process.

Whether it's SoundCloud or a new entrant, by utilizing the Blockchain to obviate much of the uncertainty around rights issues, an entire new wave of applications and investment could emerge in the music space.

BLOCKCHAIN TECHNOLOGY IS OUR CHANCE TO REBUILD THE INTERNET IN A WAY THAT BENEFITS CREATORS

Aug 12, 2015

On "Cuyahoga," a track from REM's great record, *Life's Rich Pageant*, Michael Stipe sings, "Let's put our heads together/start a new country up." It's an evocative image that Stipe employs to compel us to reconsider not only the trajectory the United States has taken since "our father's father's father" tried to "erase the parts he didn't like," but also what we would do differently if given the opportunity.

A similar question is currently upon us with respect to the Internet. What if we could reimagine the Internet—put our heads together and erase the parts we don't like—and start again? What would we do? What would we change?

Blockchain technology could play a key role in this reinvention.

The promise of the Internet, and—as the still-definitive text on the Internet, *The Cluetrain Manifesto*, states—the reason it was the fastest-adopted technology since fire is that it allowed people whose voices had been silenced to reclaim them—to tell their stories.

This reclamation of voice and sharing of stories has truly fueled the Internet to this point. Certainly, as I've discussed, many of our more prurient voices and stories have shaped the technology, but—at its core—we still come online in order to share and connect.

The issue now is that our stories—whether told in the form of song, text, photos, tweets, blog posts, etc.—have become both our currency and our source of identity.

Never has it been more important than to be the "patient zero" of a meme that goes viral; to coin a phrase that becomes part of the vernacular; to be the first to write, sing, paint, or otherwise express something that establishes you as a "creative," a thought or key opinion leader.

For those who get there first, they are rewarded with book deals, TED talks, inbound traffic, offers to provide commentary, etc. Those who get there second or later await the fate worse than anything else on the Internet: indifference. A Facebook post that no one Likes.

This crushing rush towards "first" has led to a scramble for verification across all sectors. We now have ludicrous discussions about whether Tweets are copyrightable. (To put it to rest: Almost without exception, they are *not* [a haiku, *perhaps*, being an exception], and even if they could be, one would have to register their copyrightable tweet prior to bringing an infringement suit.) Beyond tweets, we now have an ongoing public back and forth about who said what first, and in what context.

Attribution is the new currency, and the stakes are high.

For all of its distribution prowess, the Internet as we know it isn't terribly good at ascribing proper attribution. Certainly, the Internet will fill a "truth" vacuum, and largely abhors information asymmetry. However, attempting to find a verified creator for much of the work that is being made and distributed at an ever-increasing pace on the Internet is far from a simple or precise process.

Can verification be accomplished with today's Internet? Perhaps. **Can finding the source of any type of intellectual property be done in a way that also provides credit, attribution, ability to use/re-use/build upon, and compensate the creator be accomplished with any type of speed or ease? Absolutely not.**

Those who developed the internet rightly focused on creating the "pipes" that give us the ability to democratize, to share, and to give back the "voice." What was not focused on was ensuring that those who create what is passed through the "pipes" are, if they so desire, credited and compensated for their contributions, and—most importantly—able to have a say on how these creations are used by others. The Reddit Revolt and other burbling sectors of discontent show that people are only willing to fill pipes that are owned or controlled by people who have a financial connection to the pipes for so long without some form of benefit—financial or credit—or control. It will not be the last of these revolts.

A central concern, therefore, of a newly-imagined Internet would be to utilize Blockchain technology to address these issues. What if, for instance, there was a Content Management System (CMS) of sorts that allowed for content creators to not only publish their work to the Internet, but also—at the same time—to register their work and the associated "rules" around their work to the Blockchain.

In this manner, the original creator would not only be on record as the creator, but—utilizing smart contracts—also determine how/if/when/and at what price their works could be used by others, and be compensated—financially or via attribution—when such use took place.

I, for instance, would love to be able to track the ways in which my articles on Blockchain and the arts—which I've been writing for some time now—have been utilized by the slew of recent articles on the subject. In such articles published in this space, I've tried to explain that Blockchain technology has the following characteristics:

- The Blockchain is a public ledger that records (providing ownership and time stamp) and validates every transaction made worldwide.
- What makes this network unique and secure is that all transactions are authorized and backed by thousands of computers (called miners), achieving consensus on each transaction.
- No one owns it (hence the term "decentralized"), and therefore it's immutable, and there is no single point of attack for those attempting to "hack" or otherwise alter the records on the Blockchain registry.
- The technology enables peer-to-peer (P2P) transaction capabilities without any involvement of a central authority or a third party.

These characteristics encourage me and others to believe that Blockchain technology may indeed allow for a fundamental redefinition of the Internet.

I recently had the opportunity to speak with some people at the leading edge of this redefinition.

Amos Meiri is one of the principals of a company called Colu. I was provided demo access to their service, which is essentially a developer's platform to facilitate the growth of products who desire to access Blockchain technology. In other words, Colu is doing the heavy lifting of actually creating the registration—irrespective of the content—on the Blockchain.

I utilized the Colu interface to create a registration on the Blockchain for a piece of artwork I created. I am now able to reference it, share it, and create some rudimentary rules around the usages of this piece of art by others.

It's all very technical at this point, and certainly far from being something the mass populous will be utilizing, but it *does work*, and there is a definite thrill about the fact that it makes something that has been largely theoretical satisfyingly real.

For those who are curious or eager to tell me that "without Bitcoin, there is no Blockchain," let me pre-empt you: Bitcoin is integrally related to Colu specifically, and the Blockchain generally. Mark Smargon, Co-Founder and VP of Product at Colu explains how they utilize Blockchain technology and Bitcoin:

"By sending Bitcoin dust (a very small number of Bitcoins) and attaching information to them, the Bitcoins are effectively

'Colored' to represent a digital asset, so you are basically not dealing with Bitcoins any more but with something else, a digital asset that has Bitcoin properties. This process is called 'Colored Coins.'"

In some respects, Colu is a few layers deep in what I refer to as the "Blockchain Stack." As a developer's platform, it lacks the top level of the stack: a "front end" or UI.

Fortunately, there are others rushing to provide this front end/UI of the stack by devising a pleasing interface for those who desire to utilize Blockchain technology.

One such company is Revelator, who today is announcing their partnership with Colu. I have known their founder Bruno Guez for many moons—he and I both ran labels that were owned by Chris Blackwell: Bruno ran Quango, while I ran Rykodisc.

I spoke to Mr. Guez recently, and he walked me through the Revelator model. Its value proposition is to help artists and others with IP by providing them access to the Blockchain via a UI, and to offer a suite of services that will provide data and other tools to these content-owners related to the usage of their works.

Thus, Colu and Revelator combined represent something of a full stack with respect to Blockchain technology, and, in so doing, may be laying foundations for a revised Internet.

Whether it will be Colu, Revelator, Imogen Heap or any number of the others feverishly attempting to create systems and protocols that leverage the decentralized registry that is the Blockchain in order to create a new type of Internet, the pace of progress in this space is quickening.

My hope is that we learn from the shortcomings of our

current Internet, and to quote Mr. Stipe again, “begin again” with a system—utilizing Blockchain technology or otherwise—where authors/creators not only have credit, but are able to provide rules both for *how* and at what price their content may be used/distributed/transformed. Otherwise, the new boss, will be the same as the old boss.

PART II

IMOGEN HEAP'S MYCELIA PROJECT

Imogen Heap's Mycelia Project

Imogen Heap's Mycelia: An Artist's Approach for a Fair Trade Music Business, Inspired by Blockchain

Imogen Heap Gets Specific About Mycelia: A Fair Trade Music Business Inspired by Blockchain

IMOGEN HEAP'S MYCELIA: AN ARTIST'S APPROACH FOR A FAIR TRADE MUSIC BUSINESS, INSPIRED BY BLOCKCHAIN

July 17, 2015

Imogen Heap is fed up with hearing artists, herself included, complain about the current state of the music industry. And when the composer, performer, technologist, inventor, and the only female artist to have ever won the Grammy for engineering decides to take action, things happen.

Ms. Heap is a galvanizing presence and a catalyst for change; the rare artist who is willing to channel her dissatisfaction into something tangible, and —given her popularity—able to have people pay attention. This spirit has resulted in, among other things, pioneering the practice of self-releasing music with 2005's *Speak for Yourself,* long before it became somewhat of the norm to do so; to wrapping each song around a different project for her 2014 album, *Sparks*; to inventing a Musical glove that she's presented at TED and other stages (and you really must see to understand.)

Via Zoe Keating, who I interviewed on the subject of Bitcoin and the Arts, I was introduced to her good friend, Ms. Heap, and recently had the opportunity to speak—via Skype (Ms. Heap lives in England) and email—with her.

After Heap's 20-year career of wading through the dense fog of the Music industry (along with every other artist on the planet), Heap's crystal-clear belief—as is mine—is that, given the unethical foundation upon which the industry was built, and its many infamous shortcomings, nothing short of a wholesale reinvention will ever lead to real change.

A big part of this change, Ms. Heap feels, will involve Cryptocurrency and Blockchain-like technology. Ms. Heap acknowledges that we're some time away from "solving" the problem, but Ms. Heap's vision—a project she refers to as Mycelia—for how this change might come about is the most fully-formed I've yet to hear from anyone.

Below is Part One of my interview with Ms. Heap, in which we discuss the motivation for Mycelia, and Ms. Heap presents a surface level overview of the concept. In part Two, Heap takes us much deeper; providing specific details of how Mycelia and its ecosystem could practically work, Future posts will bring in other voices and ideas around this.

Watch this space, Imogen Heap is primed, and it's about to get interesting.

[The interview has been edited for grammar and clarity, and I have added emphasis via bolding certain passages, but, otherwise, it is presented unaltered.]

George Howard: Tell me about your motivation for this project?

Imogen Heap: It's time to turn the music industry on its feet. I say that, as it's always been topsy-turvy. The record industry built its foundation upon the blues and jazz of predominantly African-

American artists, who were not given the best deals for anything at the time... never mind record deals! Their pockets were the last thing on the dealmakers' minds. Lawyers and accountants made the decisions, and built contracts entirely around bringing the big guns the most amount of money, and the artists the least (if any at all). These founding artists were given a shockingly bad deal, and ever since artists have been struggling to have their voice heard.

Combined with this, the industry wasn't birthed in our digital age where online databases and flow of information are the norm. It's adopted technology in various forms along the way that invariably didn't fit with what came before; and, as a result, it's become more and more fragmented. It's ultimately gotten itself into a right angle.

Now it feels as if the music industry is a complete mess: a rusty, overstretched, tired machine. Grappling with a lot of old, crooked contracts that don't reflect our times, music services that run on greed to please shareholders smothered in buy-buy-buy adverts, dated accounting setups favoring anyone but the artist thanks to gross inefficiencies, confusing royalty statements and delayed payments (if any at all), coupled with the music itself not always being tagged effectively, and thus leading to mistakes...plus patchy copyright databases. It is almost impossible to find out who REALLY gets what.

I've lost sleep in the past, scratching my head over the small print, with an icky feeling maybe I was selling my soul to do what I love. And, at the end of it all, more times than not, we are listening to seriously degraded quality sound files, on tiny speakers or trendy hyped-up headphones lacking quality sound. Artists and music deserve better.

GH: It makes me think of the Tom Waits quote about contracts, "The large print giveth, and the small print taketh away." So, what do we do?

IH: We need to begin again. With the artists and their music at the start and heart of their industries' future landscape. It's the only way. There is little to be kept, yet a lot to learn from the hotchpotch of services present today—from labels to distribution mechanisms.

We need to cut out the middlemen, of which, in the music industry, there are way more of them than there are artists; one reason perhaps why it is such a struggle to create a fair platform for artists from within the current landscape. Music needs to breathe and so do the music makers.

GH: Completely with you with respect to cutting out the middlemen. That's why my partners and I started TuneCore and now Music Audience Exchange. But, can artists do it on their own? How do we make it breathe? You're living this scenario. You have a new song ready to release, with more in the pipeline. How are you confronting this?

IH: If only I had all the answers... Lots of people are working on these issues, and coming up with novel ways to navigate and work within this topsy-turvy music world, but there's so much wasted energy as it's building upon something so inefficient.

I have a new song, "Tiny Human," that I was planning to release, but I just felt like I was going to be adding to my gripes rather than moving anything forward. The current options on HOW to go about releasing a song fills me with dread and really puts me off. It's SO complicated and time consuming, and largely unclear who gets what and why. I want to find a real solution and release music commercially again, with confidence, once I have. That could take years, but I'm at a good point in my life to do it (maybe also being a new mum brings out the bigger picture yearnings), and feel it's absolutely worth it in the long run.

So, I thought: I'll put myself in the shoes of an unsigned act with no management and reimagine things a bit.... and when I do, I dream of a kind of Fair Trade for music environment with a simple one-stop-shop-portal to upload my freshly recorded music, verified and stamped, into the world, with the confidence I'm getting the best deal out there, without having to get lawyers involved.

GH: I should add a bit of a disclosure here. While I am an associate professor at Berklee College of Music, and reviewed early drafts of the recently-issued study entitled, "Fair Music: Transparency and Money Flows in the Music Industry" I am not one of the authors. It is timely, but coincidental that Ms. Heap's and my discussion took place around the release of the Berklee study and that both Ms. Heap and the authors of the Berklee study emphasize the word "Fair" in their respective works and thinking.

IH: In one sense, my music, old and new, is reaching and being enjoyed by more people than ever, and of course this is the most incredible gift—to connect... but that music, in itself, doesn't generate a fair income and reflect this growth. I'm more popular than ever but I'm earning less cash from the music itself. What's up with that? If I can't make that part of it work, what hope is there for someone thinking about music-making as a career?

There are of course other revenue streams which bring in cash for artists, such as brand sponsorship or patronage as I see it (my new song "Tiny Human" for example, set to become Mycelia's test case, is the new Sennheiser campaign song), film or TV syncs, merchandise, live performances or giving talks and workshops, etc.

Not everyone is going to be able to sustain themselves with these alone (and you'd have to be an established artist to do so on the most part.)

Shouldn't we, at the very least, be able to make music and derive a fair amount of pay, directly linked to that? It also always feels as if there has to be a clever business plan or marketing strategy to earn money from the music we make.

GH: Right, right. This isn't talked about enough. **We tell artists to do everything; be the artist *and* the business person. Something gives.** The best I can come up with is that efficiencies via technology might facilitate this. You mentioned the idea of uploading your new music so that it's verified and stamped. Does this lead us to the Blockchain?

IH: It's all been so wrong but it could now be so right. The combination of the technology being here and the music-loving public, now mostly aware of how unfair the rates and deals are for the artists they love and how unsustainable it is, I think leads us into a very exciting era for music (and all artists of creative content for that matter, from writers to photographers.)

My wandering mind looks to the future, and—as I'm pretty much free of all publishing, management and record contracts (still working on one label) for the first time since I was 17—I'm in a really good position to try stuff out. I need to start again—afresh, to be outside the box, and live the change. I'm hugely passionate about helping to bring a service… a system—something deeply elegant and beautiful to light.

It's restructuring, not shunning all which is available today. Enabling record labels and streaming services—who aren't all bad, to say the least, and who still will, of course, have a valid and much needed place in this new landscape—to find, nurture and be a beacon for artists, but in a fair environment.

For years, I've been so frustrated with the deep opacity of the music industry stopping me from really making the most out of my career and connecting the dots. The 'black boxes,' the NDAs, the endless contracts and statements. In the last few years, auditing labels and publishers seems to have become the norm, as it's apparent how consistently the books don't match up. You can pretty much guarantee you'll find something, but it's not always intentional; it's just the deals, trigger points, and percentages are so complex—even more when mergers and acquisitions occur—that it's hard to get it right every time, if you're human!

BUT if you're a computer program, a piece of software, a database… these issues disappear as it's just math half the time. This bit goes to this person, this bit to that person, etc., and it doesn't take a year to reach the artist/writer/performer… it's instant because it's automated.

On top of this, culture-shifting new music distribution services gather really useful data from artists' fans which could massively help us be more efficient… if it was open, gathered and presented in the right way, but so much of it's not offered up for analysis.

GH: So, is this a moment of—as they say—"creative destruction," where the old system can finally be overturned to make room for a new system? Because, **systems built upon firmaments of unethical behavior—eventually—falter?**

IH: Maybe within five years from now, yes, I feel the system will fail, as artists will leave this complicated landscape, with little feedback and clarity for a better alternative. A fair, true, bright and shining home for music that will have quietly been rising up from the breaking bones of this love to hate by many, Music Industry. I call this place, **Mycelia** (it helps me to have a name, like a song, to jam ideas into).

GH: Tell me about it?

IH: It dawned on me a few months ago that the mechanism to create and sustain a place like Mycelia exists now with the help of Blockchain technology and crypto-currencies. I am for the first time EVER, really excited and positive for the future of music and its industry; for artists old and (more importantly) new, along with the hyper-enriched feedback loops that could exist with their listeners, collaborators and flag-wavers. The FLOW of creativity, collaboration, storytelling and connecting on so many levels is going to change big time, save time... and just in time!

Its success will come from the adoption of millions of music-lovers. A grand-scale ongoing, collective project like no other. To document, protect and share that which we love, and build a place for it to grow, enabling future generations of artists to blossom as well as honoring those of the past.

Open source: a living, breathing, smart, decentralized, transparent, adaptable, useful, shining home for our love of music. A home which allows creativity to flow, connect and facilitate collaboration on so many levels, many of which just haven't been possible. With this grand library of all music comes the formation of the basis upon which all music businesses from digital radio to tour bookings can then grow and thrive from. Empowering the artists, turning and landing the industry finally on its feet.

Inspired by the largest living organisms on earth, ancient, unseen, core to life itself, Mycelium (plural Mycelia) can stretch for miles, beneath the surface. Each artist acting like its own Mycelium, in full, animated dialogue with others on the global network.

Mycelia is huge, as it holds all music-related information ever recorded anywhere ever ever *ever*, but this organism stretches across our planet between hundreds of thousands of personal computers. It is the world's greatest and most treasured library, and it belongs to the two collective parties who solely make music complete: the music makers and their audience.

In our next interview, Ms. Heap discusses specifics around Mycelia, where it starts to really come to life.

IMOGEN HEAP GETS SPECIFIC ABOUT MYCELIA: A FAIR TRADE MUSIC BUSINESS INSPIRED BY BLOCKCHAIN

Jul 28, 2015

Imogen Heap and I recently had a free-wheeling discussion on the future of the music business, Cryptocurrency, and her most recent innovation: an idea she refers to as Mycelia. In Part One of our Interview, Ms. Heap discussed the problems endemic to the music business that have led her to muse upon Mycelia.

Here, in Part Two of our conversation, Ms. Heap presents an expansive view on the challenges and opportunities facing the music industry and artists, and provides specifics about her vision for Mycelia.

[The interview has been edited for grammar and clarity, and I have added emphasis via bolding certain passages, but, otherwise, it is presented unaltered.]

George Howard: So, Imogen, where are you currently with Mycelia?

Imogen Heap: Mycelia is a working idea space for me, an artist who is searching for a sustainable future for music. It's not a project that I'm actively bringing to life just yet. I'm more sharing the idea to see what pops up from having put the word and ideas out there.

So often, platforms get built without any artists being involved at all (which is rather ridiculous), but I really want to get involved and add to the conversation, in the hope of us collectively finding one true home for music.

I don't offer all the answers, of course. I'm not a coder or a systems developer, but I'm dreaming more the flow of how I feel logically the system needs to work. There are no businesses currently in our existing chain of music business workings that get wiped out [by Mycelia], but more the way in which they operate, and thus leaving the creative sides of the business to operate freely and without their clunky counterparts.

There are ever-increasing platforms that need *our* music in order to survive, and I feel it should happen the other way around: The artist uploading one true version of their content, and all services point to that one. Nice and simple!

GH: Yes. This idea of services *using* artists' work without the artists having control or deriving any discernable benefit (monetary or promotional), while the owners of these sites benefit, prompted me to write the piece, "Does the Reddit Revolt Foretell a Similar Uprising for The Music Business?"

IH: Right. More and more (and especially since Part One of our conversation was published), I'm finding people on similar wavelengths, and am greatly encouraged that actually a Mycelia-like place isn't too far away after all. Some people are even halfway to building one.

GH: That's exciting to hear. Before we get to that, I want to get some more details about your vision for Mycelia. When you talk about Mycelia, you use the analogy of spores. Can you elaborate?

IH: Mycelia—the system/library/database—hosts hundreds of millions of Spores, which hold the creative content. In this case, music and its related data (but not limited to Music, as I see this as a model for all creative content, and Mycelia would benefit hugely from their living together).

Upon their collective foundation, the services—that both the artists and those who engage with it so desperately need—can grow above ground. These services I refer to as "Mushrooms."

Those which are taxing, inefficient or "closed," as they do in nature, are rejected, wither and die. A hashtag, linked to each Spore, tracks its movements, and keeps its trail intact on the Blockchain, while the Spore itself is updated, as and when new information is added or swapped out (a better-quality version for instance).

This enables one true instance of the creative content to live in Mycelia. This Spore, verified by the content creator, is then used by all services "looking" for it. The Spore contains all information the artist can and wishes to input. The more elaborate and detailed, the more fun and useful the services can be when pulling data from within it. **So essentially, embedded within the Spore are "rules" as to who can do what with it, when, and how.**

GH: Sounds ideal. How do artists get paid?

IH: On Mycelia, we mostly share and stream the Spores, and though fewer people need to these days—as hard disk space becomes mostly redundant as we stream from "the cloud" or "the Mycelial network"—you can still download.

Whenever the Spore is interacted with, the payment is distributed as the creator sees fit. The music distribution and the payment mechanism are entwined, and so whether the music is "on tap" or attached to a subscription-based model, every play is accounted for and directly goes to the artist from the person listening. For example, it could either be free (for a limited time maybe, until you decided to change it) or a micropayment could be sent directly into the creator's digital wallet every time it's interacted with.

Attached to the Spore are instructions to pay x, y, and z, and the verified copyright owner would denote who gets what. Currently labels, publishers, collections societies, etc. do this for the featured artists and musicians, but in Mycelia, this is done directly, saving time and money for all involved.

GH: The key is transparency?

IH: On Mycelia, all this data could be transparent. Though some artists may choose to hide how the payments get split, others may see it as a chance to promote the integrity of the content within the

Spore. There would need to be a clever layer of opacity (something like a Bitcoin tumbler effect perhaps?) at the final payment end to protect the identities of the digital wallets' owners, as this could easily lead them open to be hacked.

I could choose to pay the guitarist, video director, my press agent, etc. a percentage of my song so the Spore credits their digital wallets accordingly when it's interacted with (listened to, shared or downloaded).

In the smart contract of the Spore, instructions could be carried out automatically, so once a certain amount is reached, contract fulfilled, the payment distribution is triggered to send to another payee or change its percentages. When a new mushroom pops up onto Mycelia, that would mean I'd need to revise my content's smart contracts. Then, I would update new software, and hey, presto… good to go.

Equally, the Spore could credit a charity, your spouse, or another artist. In this way Artists can act like beacons or patrons for other artists or charities.

Also, in our decentralized Mycelia, it's only in existence thanks to everyone hosting and updating the network of Spores, and so those who play their part equally get rewarded.

GH: Is this similar to Bitcoin mining?

IH: I have been chatting to some of the guys at Ethereum, and the word on the (Shoreditch) street is that the way mining is currently carried out isn't sustainable for the long-term future of the Blockchain. [Ethereum] have some novel ways to get around this and I will leave it to Vinay Gupta, one of their members, to do the talking, as I know you're going to be interviewing some of the guys who I'm in talks with next.

But in regards to incentivizing people to tend to Mycelia, yes: Mycelians (is this getting ridiculous!?) who actively and systematically verify and police the integrity of the data, get paid. A standard transaction fee will be paid as part of the movement of data and this would also go to the "miners/librarians." This is a payment of trust also, as Mycelia's librarians are a much-appreciated bunch, who would get perks all the time.

Artists may choose to encourage extra care and attention in offering from, say, concert tickets, a private dinner or a handmade Christmas card...whatever the artists would like to offer. If and when "mining" specifically ever becomes defunct, as a new way to verify and compact Blockchain transactions becomes possible, then, perhaps, that same percentage could go to a "support new artists pot," for example—kind of like a record company advance.

All decisions will be made collectively by a vote from the content creators. The spores may also be updated by an "unofficial source." If the artist allows, concert dates, setlists, audience photos, blogs, etc. could be added. That spore can have preferences turned on or off by those engaging with it to show whether it's official (the content creator) or fan-added material (where they would also, in turn, become a content creator and the artist can become their fan.)

I have this 'preferences' feature on my new website because those who complete the role of music (the listeners) hold the other half of its story. It is also tag-based and only as good as its content (which is growing slowly,) so perhaps almost a pre-cursor to Mycelia in how one could search and cross reference.

On Mycelia, everyone is both a maker and a player. Therefore, Mycelia is not limited to music. It's all creative media, and not restricted to professional music makers/songwriters.

But money isn't all that you can earn on Mycelia. You can be rated by all kinds of things—from creativity to your social media reach. These ratings would go with you wherever your content is viewed (either directly from the library of Mycelia or one of the Mushrooms.) This enables anyone, in turn, to become a "professional," as content speaks for itself.

So, no multiple versions of you on Mycelia (like in Twitter/YouTube/Facebook), but one identity; your wallet linked where you virtually "exist," and all Mushrooms pull the relevant information from here.

Simply put, no matter who you are, if your data is being used, you'll be acknowledged by Mycelia's ratings and/or paid for it. So, if you are high-up in efficiency and trustworthiness, but don't have that much of a social reach yet, you may be cheaper than a Pro with a following, but you can still get started.

GH: So, what about today's big buzzword of "curation" then, won't this just create chaos?

IH: Well, the Mushrooms are where Mycelia really comes to life, as without them it is essentially a massive library with no curation! The Mushrooms (or services) are the YouTube, Spotify, SongKick and Soundclouds on Mycelia.

As they are equally sharing and giving information, they get paid in a similar way, being dependent on their listener or viewership size. Those which curate, visualize and map the Spores' content with flair while connecting their 'data dots,' will be successful.

This means that those which are useful for the artist and listener alike, will survive, as artists (and users) could pay them for the service directly (rather than the other way around today, where the artists are almost like an afterthought and given scraps in comparison to the big profits made by some of the larger labels and services who exist purely from their wares.)

GH: One thing that's lacking in digital files—and no one has successfully dealt with it—are things like artwork/liner notes. Does Mycelia accommodate this?

IH: Current services are so limited; generally, only giving a front cover, and, if you're lucky, some correct credit information.

Most artwork and liner notes get completely lost in the sea of digitally-distributed music, and so with it, copyright information, the musicians, instruments (and makes), writers, producer, engineer, studio, the website, contact info, thanks, etc.

Imagine having every Spore containing this information. With this information, one could develop a Mushroom to fly

you through all this information, and you could go on some amazing knowledge trails. You may find all your favorite songs have the same producer, or discover an engineer. You could listen, for instance, to the music with the artists' biography up to that point in his or her career, or see photographs from that era coupled with related news articles from that time, or just simply sit and pore over some old forgotten vinyl artwork.

Streemliner have a brilliant thing going on in this domain. They are working to get all physical packaging documented for us to engage with online (I have my last two albums digitally released in this way). Reviving lost artwork in our digital age; this would be one of my first choice Mushrooms when the time came!

GH: So, the same could be applied to other pieces of information—photos, videos, etc., right?

IH: Yes, a Spore can "contain" (but actually point to) related videos from the official music video to connected making-of clips, interviews and photos—all tagged within the spore to be cross referenced.

Derivatives too... remixes and reworks. These would all point back to the "genesis track," as say "genesis blocks" do on the Blockchain; forking off and creating more branches, mapping its journey as it goes for all who are curious to see and research the life of a song. Some works may span across decades or even a whole century. Each derivative would create a new Spore and "hash," which are documented on the Block-

chain and divvy up the proceeds accordingly.

GH: Same general idea as curation. What about marketing? How do artists stand out?

IH: Spores also act like a strand of the artist's DNA; sharing his or her favorite artists or brands, painters, authors, dancers, photographers... whatever they choose. Spreading the net, and, again, **connecting the dots.**

A Mushroom could pop up to enable brands to connect to artists, and *vice versa.* Say someone like Ecover or the RSPCA were looking for an artist to write their next campaign song; they could search for artists who use Ecover's products or artists who support the RSPCA, and get in touch and, hey, presto...both parties are happy.

Music festivals could be sponsored in this way by brands finding a collection of artists to play who like their stuff and wouldn't mind a spot of cross-promotion.

Or, what If I was looking for ideas on who to collaborate with and could search for artists like Imogen Heap? I know I'd be able to get in contact, and know I may have half a chance. Artists could get on a tour this way or find their own support act.

Equally, fans could see which artists like other artists, and a Mushroom could grow on to Mycelia to enable listeners to listen to a real Imogen Heap radio—not just what an algorithm thinks I'd like, or someone else deciding what fans of mine would like.

In short, the artists become beacons to connect with what inspires them, and to shine a light on that may which inspire others. So much fun to be had in the Mushroom world and I'd love to be a part of building those spaces. Here, as you may gather, is where companies can make money on Mycelia.

GH: And through this marketing/connection, we come full circle, right? Now we're back to collaborations, licensing, etc.?

IH: Yes. In the Spore could sit a contract stating what the artist will allow/not allow. Perhaps even pre-cleared music under certain circumstances, making it much easier for people to use music in their films or adverts (if the artist chooses to), or just a click away from seeing the terms.

It's so hard to find who to contact if you want to use that piece of music in an advert, or remix it for example. This is often a major chore and hurdle for creatives/companies wanting to sync music to picture; preventing what could be a big earner for artists and songwriters. One good sync could pay for an artist's next album! Maybe even the song 'worth' or 'license fee' could be generated by a market place where the popularity of a track in a certain area could determine how much a company needs to pay for it?

Then the artist can accept or not/add extra if it's worth more to them, but it's a good starting point. Equally, companies could choose tracks they love, but which have no popularity. They get them cheaper, but, in so doing, drive up the price of the next one, as its reach and influence is in turn tracked.

GH: So, tons of collaborations, licenses—all in theory transparent—but also just a pile of data. How do people sift through it?

IH: So much data… but if it's ugly and clunky to navigate around, no-one will enjoy using it. No more spreadsheet-like platforms, please. I want to flow through data and knowledge and discover hidden music and other artful gems amongst the Mushrooms with gorgeous data visualization.

GH: But even with this visualization, it's still very one-sided. How to address?

IH: Feedback…This is one thing we are hugely lacking in these days. So much useful data out there is just being hidden or lost.

Imagine if there was, for instance, a Mushroom where the fans were busy raising money for your next show, and said Mushroom worked out a tour and a routing for you based on the heat map of your songs in relation to the world at large. You may find interesting pockets of fandom! Discover you're huge in Madagascar, and book your next holiday to coincide with your next gig!

Every author has a dashboard for where, when and how their content is being interacted with. The ultimate statement of affairs.

A simple "bring artist to my town" pay-in-advance ticket button attaches onto the Spore in one Mushroom. That could,

in turn, trigger a notification to the artist once thresholds had reached 100 or 1000 from individual towns. It could read: "Rio wants you to come play! 1000 audience guaranteed." You could have the option to "find sponsor," "put extra tickets on sale for larger venue," "find other artists to share costs," such as equipment or production manager.

You get the idea. If all data is open, then Mushrooms will enable Spores, Artists, and listeners to cross reference and visualize data in exciting, new, meaningful and useful ways.

GH: What's the incentive for people to contribute?

IH: Outside of ratings, or perks direct from the author there could be ways to affect the physical world, and connect deeply there too. If in your Spore you, for instance, mentioned where you wrote that song, then perhaps a struggling coffee shop could re-emerge as a hotspot for inspiration and put itself on the map…literally.

It could be that a coffee shop owner who plays an album of mine all day long and "turns people over" somehow gets a big tip from me! Fans on Mycelia could help artists organize or get the most out of all this feedback on Mycelia, and, equally, a Mushroom could offer this service, kind of like a virtual manager, by dealing with requests on your behalf, or acting upon your guidelines embedded within the Spore, and eventually earning themselves a split—once they'd proved themselves to be a good manager, promoter, or marketing advisor, and ultimately being hired in the "real world."

GH: So… a real holistic approach to the entire circle of music-related business and jobs! What about the impact of music quality?

IH: Soon enough there will be no need to download a compressed music file. The quality will be as good as when it left the mastering studio. Old crushed audio could be replaced and updated to all owners of that Spore automatically—just as updates do of software onto our computers. However, the sound will still only be as good as your headphones or speakers!

Artists/rights owners will need to put their digital verification stamp on it (as say twitter does for official accounts). People, should they want to, will know they are listening to the definite recording as the artist wished it to be heard. They could even give listening tips or hints like… "dim lights, think of your childhood sweetheart."

An idea a good friend of mine, Nick Ryan had, was that every time a Mycelia track was played by a service, a little light would come on the player to let the listener know they are playing Fair Trade Music. Simple and elegant!

You can be driving in your car and see that that Digital Radio service is currently streaming from Mycelia, and feel that little bit better perhaps knowing the artist is getting paid directly for that play rather than a fraction of the amount in a year's time from that moment… which is almost the current state of affairs! This would encourage existing services to do the switch.

GH: It's such an important vision, and I feel like every day that goes by not only emphasizes the need for this to become reality, but also seems to hint that it could come sooner than we think. Since you and I began talking about this – not very long ago – what observations have you had?

IH: Well, George, a week has now passed, during which time I have met with people on this topic, and read many online responses to the first post—iincluding the interview you did with Andy Weissman where he discusses his music "Nirvana State."

In that interview, he eloquently and succinctly (not my forte!) explains the core ideas of a Mycelia-like place; specifically regarding how rules written into the Blockchain can enable a music service to be built upon it. The key element to turning the music industry finally on its feet is to begin with the artists, and how they choose to have their music "played."

One of the meetings I've had since Part One was published, was with two people—Rupert Hine (a dear friend) and Alan Graham—behind an intriguing, immediate solution for a lot of license holders' payment and rights issues (including user-generated content.) They call it OCL, and I do believe this could be a gateway to a Mycelia of the future, which could then perhaps exist as a Mushroom.

It is a hybridized-centralized/decentralized system that is meant to build a bridge between the legacy systems of the past, and what rights owners and citizens need for the future. It entirely depends on gathering thousands of artists' support (as Mycelia would need to do as well) and, with them, starting to build a fluid, global connectivity from within our current music business to engage and empower artists, in real world and much-needed policy changes along the way.

So, rather than it being a wipe-the-slate-clean-and-start-again approach (which I initially felt was the only way due to the mess everything is in), encouragingly, I see, via their technology, how a lot of artists and musicians—especially those stuck in deals of today and yesterday—can transition into a Mycelial future.

GH: So, Imogen, what are your next steps?

IH: Just in these last few months—since I've been actively talking and sharing ideas with people—I now find myself in touch with at least five independent groups of people developing their own systems. These are just those who've reached out, but I imagine there must be more. And, since our first Forbes piece, many other people have reached out who want to help Mycelia come to life in some way—including, of course, lots of artists.

While this is really exciting—as we are all on the same page—it is a little overwhelming, and I would like to call a summit for our future home for music. We all have a common goal, and it would really make sense to pool our knowledge, technology and ideas together, let go and birth one incredible place.

GH: I love that idea! I'm in.

IH: I will post details of the summit here on my website, where people can also comment on these thoughts. On top of this, I hope to release my next song, "Tiny Human," as an art project both online and in a gallery in London. I'd like to visualize Mycelia and enable people to explore Tiny Human's Spore and how it may interact with a few example Mushrooms. I'm a bit reticent to say (as I may not manage it!), but I'd love this to happen end of September.

Finally, thank you George for this opportunity to get the word out there!

GH: Thank you, Imogen.

PART III

ARTIST INTERVIEWS

Bitcoin and the Arts: An Interview with Artist and Composer, Zoe Keating

'Bitcoin For Rock Stars' A Year Later: An Update From D.A. Wallach On Blockchain And the Arts Part 1

D.A. Wallach On Spotify, Bitcoin, And A More Moral Music Industry

Ryan Leslie's Plan To Disrupt The Music Business: Enable Artists—Not Apple—To Own Their Audience

BITCOIN AND THE ARTS: AN INTERVIEW WITH ARTIST AND COMPOSER, ZOE KEATING

Jun 5, 2015

I've now written two columns focusing on crypto currency (dominantly Bitcoin) and its potential utilization in the arts generally, and music specifically, to engender better tracking and transparency.

These articles have generated conversation, but I'm left with a strong sense that—while many people (a lot of whom profess to be experts) have very strong ideas and opinions about the relative merits and possibilities of crypto currency—there are depressingly few direct examples of the utilization of this technology affecting change with respect to transparency or accounting in art/music.

What compounds the difficulty in terms of pinpointing use cases is that—unlike other emergent technologies (Virtual Reality, etc.), crypto-currencies (mostly Bitcoin) are aggressively traded. As such, many thoughts put forward with respect to usages (current or imagined) must be viewed skeptically. One must wonder, for instance, if the person who champions a particular currency-related use case is doing so because he stands to financially benefit; i.e. they might be holding a lot of Bitcoins.

All caveats aside, my enthusiasm for Cryptocurrency remains high, even while specifics around use cases in the arts is cloudy. I thought it wise therefore to bring in another voice—a voice I know to be transparent and trustworthy—to the conversation to discuss this topic.

Zoe Keating is not only a fine musician/composer ("Into the Trees", Ms. Keating's SoundCloud postings), but also an artist who has embraced transparency around her music more so than any artist I know. For example, Ms. Keating frequently posts detailed royalty statements that allow people to see unvarnished accountings.

I imagine it's this combination of musical brilliance and the embracing of technology/transparency that led Ms. Keating to being invited to The Blockchain Summit held at Richard Branson's Necker Island.

I asked Ms. Keating some questions about this experience, and her thoughts on crypto generally, and her responses (edited only for grammar and clarity) are below. I urge you to read the entirety of Ms. Keating's responses; they are the most clearly articulated on this topic I've yet to see.

In the interest of disclosure, I have known Zoe for a number of years, and we did work together on one project several years ago with the composer Mark Isham.

George Howard: What were your overall impressions of the event?

Zoe Keating: My fly-on-the-wall impression was of a passionately engaged group of people—entrepreneurs, investors and thinkers—brought together to explore the potential of the Blockchain for the betterment of the world. Yes, they also had a cracking good time on a private island.

I certainly picked the brains of everyone who would tolerate me, and the topics were broad. Everything from encoding personal identity and property rights into the Blockchain to making elections transparent.

Hernando de Soto was a standout. His book *The Mystery of Capital* was most talked about. Bill Tai loaned me his copy to read on the beach while I was there.

GH: You've been a massive proponent of transparency—going so far as to post your royalty statements. Why do you do this, and what impact has it had?

ZK: I think because I am outside the music industry, much of the way it operates seems absurd to me, so I talk about it. I just always want to make things better and I don't know if I've had any impact, but I do it because I just feel obligated to help.

I just believe in transparency in everything and I've put my career outside the mainstream so that I can operate on my own terms. I've managed to avoid working with record labels for my entire career.

I initially published my digital music earnings because the dominant story in the press on artist earnings did not reflect my reality, nor that of musical friends I talked to. None of us were concerned about file sharing/piracy, we seemed to sell plenty of music directly to listeners via pay-what-you-want services while at the same time earning very little from streaming.

Since artists under record contracts might be prohibited from publishing their earnings, or might not even know them, I felt obliged to raise my hand and describe my reality. I thought, how can we build a future ecosystem without knowing how the current one actually works?

I expected other unaffiliated artists in my position would do the same, and we could help forward the discussion. However, I found that just like record labels, unaffiliated artists don't always want transparency either. Why? Because, across the board, from the bottom to the top, the music industry is built on people pretending to be bigger than they really are.

At the same time, other than hit songs, it is near impossible to know what the real popularity of a piece of music is. Nielsen recognized this and added streams to SoundScan rankings, but the internet is far more interesting than that.

What about popularity by "use?" To use myself as an example again, there are to date 15,000 videos on YouTube with my music in them, none of them by me. The videos are other people's unlicensed dance performances, commercial films, TV shows, student films, experimental films, art projects, soundtracks to gaming session, etc. But currently there is no way to leverage that kind of enthusiasm. Only YouTube knows how popular my music is for unauthorized soundtracks.

I'm interested in using the Blockchain to track derivative works. What if you could know the actual reach of something? It seems like there are entire ecosystems not being leveraged or monetized.

Copyright metadata is just a way to identify who should be

paid, and today that is the songwriter and the publisher. It can be surprisingly hard to find out who owns a song, let alone get permission to use it for anything.

If there was a distributed ledger of music metadata, it could keep track not only who created what, but who else was materially involved, from the producer, to the side musicians, to the people who promote it, to the samples taken from another song.

I can imagine a ledger of all that information and an ecosystem of killer apps to visualize usage and relationships. I can imagine a music exchange where the real value of a song could be calculated on the fly. I can imagine instant, frictionless micropayments and the ability to pay collaborators and investors in future earnings without it being an accounting nightmare, and without having to divert money through blackbox entities like ASCAP or the AFM.

Old school record contracts are essentially a way to pay all those entities upfront because there is no easy way to calculate and pay micro-payments into the distant future.

We've come far in dismantling that system, but have yet to replace it with anything, and that, I think, is where the pain and suffering of artists lies. Right now, we have a diminished record label investment engine, yet limited ways to compensate all the parties involved in making something.

I can imagine all this. I've been imagining it. I'm sure other people imagine it. But it's still a dream. I don't know who can do it or if anyone is doing it and yeah, the technical details are a fucking bitch. But so what? I just think there hasn't been

enough incentive in the music industry, everyone is busy fighting to keep what they already have and what initiative there is has been embarrassingly misguided (TIDAL??? WTF?!).

GH: Do you know of (either from this event or from your own experiences) of examples of artists (in any medium) utilizing crypto? If so, please describe. If not, why not?

ZK: I know Imogen Heap is trying to figure out how to make derivative works (i.e. sampling) and covers both easier to manage, paperwork-wise for her and her fans, and how to share in the success of those works. Last I talked to her last month she was investigating the idea of a music Blockchain and/or a new file format.

GH: Do you have a vision for how crypto might impact the artistic realms moving forward? Will you be embracing it if you're not now?

ZK: I tend to get excited about anything that has potential to put money and power back into the hands of individuals rather than institutions. I'm interested in enabling the musical middle class, just like I'm interested in the fortunes of the middle class at large. I don't believe that rich vs. poor has to be the only outcome in the music industry.

Like you've already written about, the corporate music establishment—i.e. record labels—have no interest in the transparency offered by Blockchain.

GH: You are an artist who has handled all of your business affairs. What guidance do you have either to other artists/business people or business people in the arts with respect to crypto/transparency, etc.

ZK: Be curious. Read. Seek out interesting people who are experts on things you know nothing about and then just enjoy each other's company. That's my whole approach to life in general.

'BITCOIN FOR ROCK STARS' A YEAR LATER: AN UPDATE FROM D.A. WALLACH ON BLOCKCHAIN AND THE ARTS PART 1

Sep 25, 2015

D.A. Wallach, the recording artist and songwriter who Kanye West and Pharrell Williams discovered while he was an undergraduate at Harvard College, wrote the article, "Bitcoin for Rockstars: How Cryptocurrency Can Revolutionize the Music Industry," in December of 2014.

Mr. Wallach's piece—eloquent, insightful, and provocative—served as the first meaningful opinion from the artist community regarding the cryptocurrency and Blockchain technology.

A lot has been written since then. I personally have explored this topic with artists like Zoe Keating, Imogen Heap, Ryan Leslie; and with Venture Capitalists and entrepreneurs, such as, Andy Weissman from Union Square Ventures, Bill Tai, Jesse Von Doom from CASH Music, and the founders of Colu.

Roughly a year from the publication of Mr. Wallach's seminal piece on this topic, I strongly believe that Blockchain technology (or some alternative distributed ledger) is the very best path forward in order to develop a music industry that enables those who create music to control their works and be compensated for their usage, and for those who desire to consume/utilize/build businesses around music to do so in a transparent and efficient manner, without self-interested in-

termediaries distorting and leveraging the process.

Pie in the sky? Perhaps, but progress is being made, and certainly no better "solutions" are presenting themselves.

I recently had the opportunity to check in with Mr. Wallach about this topic, and, over the course of a lengthy conversation, we discussed not only his views on the progress made with respect to Blockchain technology and musicians, but also his work with Spotify, and his strong conviction that there is a more moral way to approach the music industry than that which currently exists.

Our conversation was direct, and at times heated, but it is abundantly clear to me that the music industry is incredibly fortunate to have someone like Mr. Wallach to help define its future.

In this first part of our conversation, presented below lightly edited for grammar and clarity, we discuss:

- How the problems of today's music industry have less to do with nefarious executives, and more to do with "poorly architected systems."
- The need for a distributed registry.
- The unlikelihood of some sort of consortium or governmental agency coming together to create a registry.
- How institutions, such as ASCAP and BMI will be reluctant to embrace these technologies, because doing so would threaten their very existence. (This is a point I made in an early article on Blockchain, entitled, "Bitcoin Can't Save The Music Industry Because the Music Indus-

try Will Resist Transparency.")

- How consent decrees and other forms of collective bargaining are hindering artist's ability to determine the usages of their works.
- Mr. Wallach's "thought experiment" on what might happen if an artist became popular—via social media, etc.—and the artist's works were played on the radio without the artist affiliating with a PRO.

I will be posting part two of our conversation, in which—among other topics—we get very specific about Mr. Wallach's work with Spotify, and his thoughts on their approach to artists.

George Howard: So, I have the pleasure today to talk to D.A. Wallach. D.A., thanks for joining me. How are you doing?

D.A. Wallach: I am doing great. Thank you.

GH: Good. So, before we dive in on the topic at hand, I want to give a little bit of an overview. You wrote an article called: "Bitcoin for Rock Stars: How Cryptocurrency Can Revolutionize the Music Industry," back in December of 2014. That article to me was really the first one that raised a lot of awareness in the artistic community about the Blockchain.

Through my own work in that area, it is an article that keeps getting referenced, which is a testament not only to how great the article is, and how well written it is; but also to you generally, and everything that you have done in the industry. So, I was wondering, before we jump in, if you could set the stage about your career and what led you to this point.

DW: Yeah. For sure. So, as my life stands today, I sort of split my time 50/50 between continuing to make music and putting out albums as a solo artist. And, with the rest of my time, I invest in early-stage technology businesses. And, going back even further, prior to Spotify, I was spending pretty much all of my time just being a career artist. So, touring and making records. That started pretty much from the day I graduated college, which was in 2007.

So, I've gone through a number of different worlds that all sort of overlap, and which brought me to the interests that I have developed in both cryptocurrency, and also in fixing some of the core infrastructure in the music business. I had started thinking about some of these issues ten years ago, when I was literally busking on the street in Boston.

GH: Yeah. I probably saw you.

DW: You may have, unfortunately. Particularly with my experience through Spotify, and from being on the other side of the table a little bit, **I gained an even more acute awareness of really how significant some of the problems were in the way that the industry functions that aren't necessarily attributable to evil-minded executives or anything nefarious; it is really just that this industry and lots of other media industries are built upon**

really poorly architected infrastructure. In fact, no one architected it; it just evolved over the past hundred years. But, it is not up to the task of today.

GH: Yeah. It's sort of an architecture of accretion.

Thank you for that introduction and context. And, it does sort of uniquely qualify you, as you've been on both sides of the table; being an artist who has had the trajectory of busking all the way up to putting records out and playing in front of a lot of people, and selling a lot of records—this all gives you context. And then investing and working with Spotify.

Frankly, I wish there were more like you. **I think that one of the main reasons the record industry sort of devolved was that there was a separation between the people who were making the music and the people who were marketing the music. And, never the twain shall meet. So, we are lucky in the artist community to have somebody like you out there—thank you for what you are doing.**

DW: That's nice. Thanks.

GH: To your point about the lack of architecture; unquestionably, the music industry did evolve through accretion. We still talk in terms that are anachronistic, in the sense that they were invented back when the music industry was invented. I mean, "mechanical royalties" was a term used when they had to come up with some way to describe taking music and mechanically reproducing it on a piano or a music box, and yet it is still a key component.

What intrigues me about the Blockchain or a decentralized registry, generally, is that maybe now we can move to one place that has a more accurate registry as well as one that is less easily corrupted by people for their own desires or for economic imperatives or what have you. Is that a fair statement?

Was that sort of your initial gesture on this or was it not?

DW: No. I don't think it was. You know, I would sort of distinguish between two separate problems that my article is attempting to address and that, to me, is clearly more two separate problems the longer I think about this. The first one is that we really need this thing. And, by "this thing," I mean that we need a central registry where we easily keep track of who creates our art and who gets paid when that art gets used.

GH: Can I interrupt you? The idea that we need a central registry.... I would say that we need a *distributed* registry, right? I think it might be helpful for people to understand the distinction.

DW: Yeah. Absolutely. I think that is the second problem.

GW: Okay. I don't mean to change your flow. I just think there is a key distinction, because there are tons of registries out there. ASCAP has a registry, Harry Fox has a registry, Sound Exchange has a registry. What I am arguing for, and I think you are too, is a registry that is decentralized. In essence, it is distributed.

DW: Sure. What I would say is that when I first started thinking about this—before I started thinking about decentralization—I was thinking about the music industry becoming global, and that is sort of a universal trend. We have one world, one culture. It doesn't make sense really to release records in different territories on different days, and things like this because the internet has brought everyone so much closer together.

And, if you can imagine a world in which the United Nations created this database and it was a free public asset and everyone used it that would be great...and I sort of wouldn't mind a single party controlling it, as long as they were trustworthy, and were sort of easy to work with, and did a basically good job on the technology side.

But, the world in which we actually seem to live in, is one in which basically no one in the media industries trust each other.

GH: Right.

DW: So, I actually view the need for decentralization here, or the opportunity for decentralization as sort of a slightly sad testament to how corrupted the media businesses are.

I mean I sort of wish that everyone could work together and form a consortium globally that did this. But, that hasn't happened. It doesn't seem like it's going to happen. It is hard to imagine what would actually make it happen.

And, that led me to the possibility that maybe the only way to do this is to actually produce a solution that will enable everyone to work together. And, that's what decentralized stuff is good at.

GH: Yeah. I'm there. So, decentralization sort of addresses both of those things. One, it obviates the bug in the ointment of if people have control they are going to utilize that control to their own ends. And, that's life.

It also allows for it to be global, as you say, and finally allows for us to be able to distribute it across anyone who wants to use it. So, it's not just in the hands of a few people.

DW: I agree. I think that you are absolutely right that people are keeping... you know, ASCAP maintains their own database; Harry Fox maintains their own database. All of these people are keeping their sort of proprietary dataset around.

GH: I am sorry to interrupt you, but, that's where their value comes from, right? That's part of the inherent problem of saying, "Hey, ASCAP open up your database." Well, if they do that they are giving away their secret sauce. They are giving away their value.

DW: You know, I think that's their perception, and, you know, they may be partly right. But my view of it—and I am not like extremist "information should be free" type of person—it's just that in this case, I don't see anyone deriving much value from having this stuff be proprietary. Sure. It is part of ASCAP's value. Yes. They have a pretty comprehensive database of their songwriters and the stuff those songwriters created. But, I really don't think that's where their value comes from in the world.

I think the reason songwriters affiliate with them is to go and effectively collective bargain on their behalf with broadcasters and other people who use music. By the way, I think that is always going to be a potentially valuable service that they can provide in the world.

GH: So, let me stop you again. I do disagree here. And, that's okay. I think that ASCAP and BMI and any of the PROs are the most likely low-hanging-fruit to be disrupted by the Blockchain.

Let me just throw a straw man out at you and you can tell me where I am wrong. And, I am probably going to work this into an article. So, I am testing it out on you today.

If you decide that this music thing is for the birds, and you don't want to do it anymore; you are going to open up a restaurant instead, right? You want to play music in your restaurant. And, you are not you; you are someone that doesn't know the ins and outs of the music business. And, you get a letter or a knock on the door from ASCAP or BMI saying, "Hey, you want music in your restaurant? Great. You need to pay us a blanket license fee and then you can play anything that's in our catalog because we've negotiated"—as you said re: collective bargaining—"we negotiated for our writers. And you say, "Alright. I understand. Great!"

And the PROs say, "By the way, if you don't purchase this blanket license, we are going to sue you."

So, what if we were in a—and I am sort of jumping ahead a little bit—but, what if you and I got together and said, we are going to find two to three hundred artists out there who have the rights to their compositions, and we are going to put it up on the Blockchain. We are going to stipulate that this music can be used by restaurants and then we are going to find three hundred of our friends that have restaurants, and say, "Hey, you want music in your restaurant? You can use this music according to the database that we used the Blockchain to create."

And the people supplying the music will set whatever reasonable price, and the people that want to use the music will decide: "yeah I am either going to pay or I am not going to pay that."

What do we need ASCAP or BMI for? Scale?

DW: Sure. The system you are proposing I find really appealing, right. And, I think at a certain level, artists shouldn't need to affiliate with one of these PRO's in order to have their music usable in the world.

GH: And, you think you have to? You can tell I have a bias against this. So, you can shoot me down at any point. But, you are right. They shouldn't. Then, there is a burden on the services—that artists have to align themselves with—to report accurately and effectively, and we both know now that none of the PROs come anywhere near that.

DW: Sure. Look, I would distinguish between two functions that the PROs provide. One, is that they keep track of who owns this stuff, and then they move them all around, right? They go and get a check from Clear Channel. They figure out how to go and split it up. You can debate whether or not they can do a fair or a good job of that, but let's assume that they do an OK job of it. So, that's one of their functions. And, the other function is this sort of collective bargaining thing.

GH: OK.

DW: The collective bargaining thing, in general, is good for artists who don't have a lot of power. And, it's potentially worse for artists that *do* have a lot of power. So, this sort of alternative PRO that you are describing is actually sort of being done right now with a lot of powerful artists in the form of this GMR: Global Music Rights.

GH: Right.

DW: Which isn't bound by the consent decrees of U.S. Congress, and so can't demand higher rates on behalf of its songwriters who are the sort of folks who you can't live without if you have a radio station.

GH: If you are the Eagles, you can say, "We are going to pull our music from ASCAP, BMI or whoever and limit our usage." And the Eagles will not let, for instance, TV shows broadcast their music without a direct license.

Tell me if I am wrong, but doing this without the Blockchain or some other decentralized registry is just building a new system that is essentially the same as the other one, but perhaps more elitist.

And, what I am looking for is one that allows for some sort of smart contracts to exist. Where I open a restaurant, but, I can just say, "OK, I like salsa music. I want that in my restaurant, and I am willing to pay $100.00 a month." And, I plug that in and my machine goes out and looks for artists that do that type of work and are willing to allow their music to be used and the machine sort of match each other up. Is that too pie in the sky?

DW: I don't think it's pie in the sky. It should work, you know, if an alien came down and created this from scratch. So, in general, I favor that approach. I think. My wish though is that artists could do whatever they want. If they want the sort of collective bargaining power of ASCAP and they want to go in with a bunch of other artists and have someone negotiate a rate for all of them that might be better than what they could negotiate on their own—more power to them. If someone doesn't want to affiliate and wants to use a sort of system that you are describing at their own rates, then they should be able to do that too. And, I think the problem right now is that artists can't do that.

GW: Right. That is the point.

DW: I have had sort of a "thought experiment" for a while that I think would be a fun stunt. Which is: imagine that you had an artist that was really hot on the internet and you had a big bidding war over them and they signed a record deal with whomever, and they didn't affiliate with a PRO. And then as soon as they get played on the radio, all over the place, they sued every station for each play.

GH: They weren't affiliated with a PRO. For the people who don't understand: If you write a song only *you* have the write to publicly perform it, which means, have your song broadcast on radio, etc. And, if you have a hit, however that might happen—via social media or whatever— and radio stations just start playing it, and you haven't affiliated with ASCAP or BMI, those radio stations are infringing upon the songwriter's right to publicly perform the song and the songwriter can sue them for infringement.

DW: Exactly. And, I don't know if this has ever happened. I don't think it has happened with a notable artist. It's an interesting way to sort of put pressure on this system. You could imagine major artists un-affiliating from ASCAP or BMI and just reclaiming their own rights.

GH: You can imagine that. But, the problem with that is, if you are Paul McCartney, and you are making lord only knows what Paul McCartney is making from public performance royalties because "Yesterday" is being played a billion times a day, you are lacking the necessary incentive to say, "I'm going to stop doing that," and pull that song from your PRO, and then negotiate directly with every radio station and therefore make more money, because it is more of a pain in the ass to do the administrative side of it.

DW: Yep. Yep.

GH: And, that's why I go back to Blockchain. With Blockchain it can be done through smart contracts and machines. Radio stations could say, "OK I've got to only play songs that the writer has checked off the box that says, 'I'm willing for my music to be played and I am willing to be paid this amount.'" And, it could be played with Bitcoin or whatever currency. It could be in micro-payments and you wouldn't have the transaction costs.

I want to direct this back to Blockchain, though I love your thought experiment.

It's been almost a year since you posted your article. What has changed in your thinking or thoughts? It must be somewhat gratifying at least to be sort of the "genesis block" of this discussion. Are you more or less optimistic about Blockchain now than you were when you wrote this? What have you learned since then?

DW: Well, I think both. What I have seen in media related to the Blockchain, and in other verticals, notably financial services, is just an incredible flurry of creativity, energy and entrepreneurial enthusiasm for decentralization and Blockchain technology. So, I think this is a technology, generally speaking, that has more of a moral component in people's minds.

So, it's not only an interesting technical solution to a pretty complex problem, but it's also brain candy. When people learn about it and go a little deeper, they feel really smart. It sort of tickles your brain because it's hard to understand. Once you figure out the puzzle, then you want to explain it to people and do something cool with it—it's gratifying in that way.

But it also is sort of accompanied by this moral weight, and this notion that this is a fundamentally different way to organize society, or to use computation to get people to do things together. I think it is a genuinely novel idea in human history.

So, I think right now we are trying to figure what to do with it. You've got a lot of people building things that are stupid, and you have people building things that are smart. And, you have people building things that are too smart and ten years away, and don't have the sort of enabling technologies in place to make them thrive.

But, my hope is that we will start seeing some usable stuff coming out of this. But, you have to zoom out and look at technology from a ten-year or twenty-year time scale. And, we are just at the very beginning of this, hopefully.

GH: Yeah. I agree. I interviewed my friend Andy Weissman, who is a venture capitalist, on this topic and he said: "Look, my job really is to envision a world that I want to live in that is three to five years away from now." So, I am with you. I am encouraged by certain people, and as I have said, I have talked a lot with Imogen Heap and others.

I am starting to see little tiny flickers of going from sort of pie in the sky things to: "You know, I think we might actually make something of that."

D.A. WALLACH ON SPOTIFY, BITCOIN, AND A MORE MORAL MUSIC INDUSTRY

Sep 30, 2015

In Part One of my interview with the musician, investor, and entrepreneur, D.A. Wallach, we discussed the "poorly architected systems" of the music industry, and how Blockchain technology could potentially resolve some of these issues via its decentralized nature and smart contracts.

In addition to the above list of accomplishments, Mr. Wallach has had a long relationship with Spotify, and was for a time their artist-in-residence.

As anyone who has had the mis/good fortune of spending any time with me, or hearing me speak at conferences, knows, I have a troubled-at-best relationship with Spotify.

That said, I do feel strongly that the vast majority of people who work not just at Spotify, but in the music industry, generally are doing so because they value art, and genuinely do not want to intentionally harm artistic creators.

In short, I believe they mirror the sentiment that I came up with and try to repeat as often and loudly as I can: More Art Equals Less War.

Given this, and—importantly—given the fact that Mr. Wallach is an artist, I was eager to get his perspective on both Spotify specifically, and the music business, generally.

While Mr. Wallach and I don't necessarily see eye-to-eye on

Spotify, one thing we resoundingly agree on is, as Mr. Wallach says: "If we want to fix the music industry, we have to get more money flowing into it."

[Our conversation below has been lightly edited for grammar and clarity, but otherwise is transcribed verbatim.]

George Howard: What is your role at Spotify? What type of work are you doing there?

D.A. Wallach: My role at Spotify is really limited now. I have put in three and a half years of really intense work there, and, my responsibility as "artist-in-residence" was really to do two things: One, to help educate the creative community about Spotify's business model, and to sort of allay peoples' terror that this was going to destroy everything, which I've never believed it would.

On the other hand, I played a more exciting, important: to be a vehicle for artists and the creative community into Spotify.

And, things that we have built at Spotify, that were sort of catalyzed by my efforts, were to sell merchandise to the fans of the product, with the ability to sell concert tickets, and increasingly the ability to derive analytics from the behavior of people who were listening to your music.

So, I was meant to be a sort of voice of artists within the company, and obviously this has been a really fraught topic. I've spoken over the past few years literally to thousands of musicians and managers and, you know, my view remains that

this is going to be a really, really fantastic development for artists and for the music industry—that's what got me involved in the first place.

GH: They are lucky to have had you. I contend that they need a lot more people like you working there. But, certainly having you is awesome.

I am very candid about my frustrations, and also with the potential possibilities of Spotify. And, I have been really transparent about it. I do think that - if it is sort of viewed as a discovery tool, and with some of the things that you have done, whether it's with merchandise or tickets—it can potentially provide value to artists. And that's a nice through-line that provides some value.

Otherwise, it *is* fairly easy to see as Spotify using the artist to get subscribers without compensating the artist fairly.

So, I am interested to hear how you see Blockchain related to this, or not. But, how do you see Spotify grow and evolve into a place where it becomes a good business, both for them and for artists?

DW: Right. I think this relates to—in some way to what you were envisioning for the future of PROs—a sort of decentralized automated infrastructure. [NOTE: In Part One of our conversation, I lay out my theory for how Blockchain technology could obviate the role of PROs by providing direct relationships between those who desire to use music (restaurants, radio stations, etc.) and music creators.]

GH: Yes.

DW: So, what Spotify is trying to create for consumers is a way of listening to music and paying for it, that [consumers] basically don't have to think about it.

GH: Got it.

DW: Just automate everything about the consumer experience. So, the idea is that right now consumers for the most part—the vast majority of people—listen to a lot of music, but they don't pay anything for it.

I look at this really, really simply and my starting point is that if we want to fix the music industry, we have to get more money flowing *into* it. So, a lot of the conversation about Spotify and live streaming and everything is about how money is shared *within* the industry, but the problem that I have always focused on is how do we get more money *into* the industry?

GH: Love it.

DW: So, for me almost axiomatically, the only way you can do that is to convince people who aren't paying a lot for music to spend more on music than they are spending right now.

GH: Which is nothing.

DW: Which is nothing.

GH: If you are starting from a baseline of zero, as you say, getting more people to pay for music is axiomatically a good thing if the distribution of those funds in a sort of reasonable way, that both allows for artists, and the companies that are trying to build businesses around them, to survive.

DW: Absolutely. And look, there are going to be competing models for how to best accomplish this. All that we can say right now is that, after four years, **nobody in the world has done a better job than Spotify of getting people to pay for subscriptions to music.**

And, the marketplace is getting more competitive. Apple is dealing with a different model without a free tier. Other people will come along and have different models, and, as an artist, I want a lot of competition, right?

GH: Yeah.

DW: And so, to your point, what I want to see is a world in which entrepreneurs are really excited to build competitive businesses in and around music.

And, when I look at Spotify and Google and Apple getting into this; what I see is that, holy cow thank God: if you are an artist you've now got the biggest technology companies in the world fighting with each other to build the most exciting mu-

sic products.

GH: Boy, I love that! I love your spirit. The cynical view… and it's not my view. I want to be clear; I am much more in line with you.

DW: Yeah. Yeah.

GH: But, the cynical view would be: that's only because people like music, and if these companies can use music as a loss-leader to compel people to buy other products—for Apple that's iPhones, for Spotify, that's maybe a video product down the road, or what have you—then, the music is just simply a loss-leader for that. The artists—they are a dime a dozen. They self-replicate.

DW: The artist, the industry at large, and record labels can take a cynical view if they want. That's our right. We create the music. We own it. If you sell it to a record label, they own it. This is everyone's right. If we take a cynical attitude, what that will mean is that people don't want to come and start businesses around music.

We as an industry either have to be welcoming or we have to be really formidable.

GH: But, wait. Who is the industry that has to be welcoming or formidable?

DW: I think it's artists. I think it's record labels. I think it's publishers. I think it's performing rights organizations.

So, when you look at the nineties, basically if you wanted to be general about the industry, the attitude was: pirating was bad. Consumers who are pirating are breaking the law. They are stealing our [the labels'] shit, which is basically true. Anyone who is building a company which helps them do that [e.g. Napster] is breaking the law, and we [labels] are going to sue them into oblivion, and we are going to make them disappear. Because ultimately, we [labels] create the music. We have the power. We can tell the consumer how they are going to listen to our stuff and how they are going to pay us and it's on our terms.

And, it didn't work.

GH: It didn't work.

DW: It was a disaster, and as a result of that, all the consumers stopped paying.

And, so we ended up with an industry that was horribly mismanaged. Where none of the consumers paid any money for music, and as a result all the money disappeared and artists don't have money. And, that's a really bad problem to have as a media business.

And so, when I got involved in Spotify, I looked at Daniel Ek and the folks who started the company and I said, "Jesus, here are some really competent, smart, enthusiastic, determined people who want to try and fix this."

And, of course, their motivation is not only fixing it as a moral solution for artists, it is because we actually can get people to pay for music again. And, if we can do that, we are going to make a ton of money too.

GH: Yeah. Which I am fine with, by the way.

At the very beginning of our conversation, we were talking about Blockchain tech, and one of the motivations there is: there is an economic incentive to be a miner and do all those other things.

I think we are really in harmony here. So, I hope I am not coming across as disagreeing with you. You have an inside advantage at Spotify that I just don't have. All I can look at is the actions. But, I have no problem—in fact, I think it's imperative—that these companies have a financial incentive.

I think the worst thing that we could do is to say that there is some sort of *noblesse oblige*; we should just do music for the public good or something like that. Then, we end up with museums and things. There has got to be an economic imperative. And that is why I go back to Blockchain.

DW: Well, let me use this as a pivot into talking about why I think streaming actually sets the stage for a sort of decentralized infrastructure. That's what we are talking about, and the reason for that is...there are two:

The first is that companies like Spotify—and this is something that I have seen from the inside—they have to manage how complex the industry is, and how fragmented the information is; it costs them a ton of money and takes up a lot of time. When we talk about an industry that welcomes entrepreneurship and innovations, I think that means we have to lower the barriers to entry, right? And, one of those barriers right now is that if you want to start up by a competitor and you are George in Boston....

GH: You have to negotiate with all the master rights holders.

DW: Oh my God! You have to deal with all this complex stuff. And then you have to find some computer genius...

GH: And deal with 7Digital or some of these master holders that are ... well ... I am not going to say what I really think, but that are challenging at best to deal with. But, go ahead.

DW: And, you have to build this insanely complicated database to deal with rights ownership and payment specs. Who do you hire to do that? These are all problems that should be non-problems. That's one.

GH: I love this. So, let's be clear—and this is what I do in my consulting business—if somebody comes in and says, **"I want to start a music streaming service," unfortunately, I have to tell them the Byzantine pathway to doing so is mired in all the transaction costs and uncertainty...and uncertainty is the worst thing for investment.**

DW: Right. But, let's talk about what a solution could look like.

Now, the other aspect of streaming music, in particular, is that—this is hotly contested but, for better or worse—the business model requires you to pay out a fraction of a cent every time people play something.

So, we are moving from an industry where a consumer buying a song for a dollar can play it forever. We say, "Look, every time you listen to something, you pay a very tiny amount and we are going to pay that out to the artist and we're going to keep a fraction of it."

What this means practically, is that the music industry as a whole, is moving towards a micro-payment based economy. Right now, we don't have the infrastructure to support that.

So, the way a company like Spotify approaches this, is you basically look every week, or every month, or every quarter, at how much stuff got played. And you say, each time it got played that was a half of a penny multiplied by the number of plays. That's the check that we are going to write every month.

And, what would be much better is if companies like Spotify—every time someone listened to a song—could instantaneously issue a micropayment. They literally can't do that today, because: how do you do it? You can't send a friend half a cent.

GH: Exactly.

DW: So, you need a financial infrastructure that allows for the flow of fractional payments in real time. And that would be a

great service to artists. It would be a great service to services like Spotify and Google and Apple.

GH: I want to talk at this point about morality. To really know where you are going with that; how Blockchain has a moral component to it? Because typically when you talk about financial tech, I think people are very skeptical about the immoral things you could do with it.

But, what you have suggested is completely in line with what I have proposed too: using a cryptocurrency to do the micro-payments and obviate those transaction costs. Do them in real time. And, here's what is important: Do it transparently.

When you have a company like Kobalt that can enter a very convoluted and crowded space and gain market share just by saying, "Hey, yeah. We are not going to lie to you," it shows you the type of demand for moral, or at least transparent procedure.

The transparency obviates so much of these unethical foundations in the music businesses.

DW: Totally. And, one thing that I have taken away from my experience with Spotify, and dealing with the record labels is that, look, the music industry has a terrible history of screwing artists and being full of evil atrocious con artists, right? But, my experience—at the highest levels of Universal Music Group, with Warner Bros., or any of these places—is that most of the people are really nice people.

GH: I totally agree.

DW: And, most of them are…it's like if you are in the United States Congress today, it's not your fault that you have to spend half of your time raising money.

GH: The system sucks. Right.

DW: The system sucks, and everybody who is involved with this is basically complicit in this thing because nobody has stepped up and created a solution.

GH: There's the moral problem and that's because they're afraid. They are afraid at the higher levels that if they step to the higher level of innovation, that you and I are talking about, they are going to get fired—and so they don't.

DW: Yeah. Hell yeah. And, also there is a more charitable view, which is that it's really hard.

GH: Of course it's hard. But that's their job!

DW: There is a reason I wrote "Bitcoin for Rock Stars", and didn't start this company. I think this is a ten-year project. You need people who are really, really capable and *maniacally* obsessed with this problem.

The state of the art now as I look at it is poised to produce the sort of solution that you and I are talking about and grasping for in general.

What I have yet to see is the right entrepreneur, approaching it in exactly the right way, and there are a bunch of folks working on parts of the problem, who are talented and really, really interesting. But, what I want to see is folks coming together, and working exhaustively to make this happen.

GH: That's what it is going to take. D.A., you've got the ball rolling. I can't thank you enough for not only writing the article, but for the work that you have done on behalf of artists. I know now having talked to you exactly where it stems from. So, we are all grateful to you for what you have done. I am grateful to you for taking the time—it was more time than you allocated, so I appreciate it. It has been wonderful to talk to you, so thank you very much.

RYAN LESLIE'S PLAN TO DISRUPT THE MUSIC BUSINESS: ENABLE ARTISTS—NOT APPLE—TO OWN THEIR AUDIENCE

Jul 21, 2015

Ryan Leslie had a problem. His first album, *Ryan Leslie*, had done very well, but even though his second album, *Transition*, received a Grammy nomination, it, and subsequent records, sold progressively fewer copies. Mr. Leslie, a prodigy (graduating from Harvard at 19) who established himself as an in-demand producer prior to releasing his first record, was confronted with a downward trajectory that showed no signs of abetting.

Faced with this reality, Mr. Leslie did something all great entrepreneurs do: He created a solution for his own problem.

This solution has not only allowed him to thrive as a musician—creating direct, authentic connections with his fans that generate far more revenue for him than he ever had signed to a label—but also led him to create a business that enables other artists to do the same.

The company is called Disruptive Multimedia, and its clients include artists like 50 Cent and Talib Kweli. Most importantly, its product—the Super Phone—is an app that musicians can use to build, engage with, and connect to fans.

Try it out. You can text Ryan at this number to see it in action: 915-600-6978.

Having been introduced to Mr. Leslie via Twitter—of

course—after I made a snarky tweet about how entrepreneurs and musicians (is there any difference?) need to stop talking and start doing, **I was delighted to finally have a real-world example of someone who has transcended the "talk" stage and has actually created something to help artists.**

This led to a free-wheeling and wide-ranging conversation with Mr. Leslie about the state of the industry, and how artists can leverage the technology that is available to them to better understand/connect with their fans. Mr. Leslie is generous with his knowledge and experience, and really does present a tangible way forward for musicians to better connect with their fans.

Bottom line: The windmill Mr. Leslie is tilting towards is enabling artists—NOT the streaming services or labels—to own their audience. I hope he hits it!

George Howard: I'm just curious, somebody who you don't know really well asks you, how did you get here? What's the story?

Ryan Leslie: The story is that, really, I grew up in a musical household, so from very early on I had a dream that I wanted to do music and make it a career. My parents being administrators in the Salvation Army, they were a little less excited about that...

GH: Where did you grow up, Ryan?

RL: I grew up all over...the Salvation Army is an organization that's run like the military, so we would move all the time. I was born in D.C., spent the first nine or so months of my life in Suriname at a children's home. My grandparents looked after me while my mom finished college, and then we honestly just moved so much. Atlanta, Kentucky, Tennessee, Virginia, Brussels, Belgium for a year.

By the time I was a junior in high school, I had gone to four different high schools. I took the Cal High School Proficiency Exam, tested out of high school in California and got into the Riverside Medical Program amongst other schools. Really applied to Harvard, Stanford, Yale as a longshot—Yale wrote back saying, "hey, we don't think you're socially developed enough," and Harvard actually accepted me.

GH: Seems like you were like 15?

RL: Yeah, super young. So, there I was: a senior at Harvard at 19, ready to embark on the world. I delivered the Harvard oration the year that I graduated, and it was a really simple message, basically...**figure out what makes you tick, what keeps you up at night, and do that, because that is how you'll actually contribute the most to the world without any coaxing from other people, or coaxing if you will from salary or anything else.**

GH: If you can turn that thing that you do when you're procrastinating what you're *supposed* to be doing into your business, then that works. I remember when I was in graduate school running my little label, and all I really wanted to be doing was stuffing envelopes with records and all that stuff, but instead I was writing papers on Faulkner. Then, it sort of dawned on me that maybe I should try to do this thing that I really want to do, that you said "keeps you up at night." I think that's a good line, and is better in some ways than the cliché "follow your dreams" or "follow your bliss" because that's so vague. If you can actually see yourself doing these things because you *are* rather than, "Oh, I'd like to be...whatever" that's a very different thing—it's much less aspirational and more tangible.

RL: I see this all the time. For folks that want to do music, I've literally met zero people in my life who don't like some form of music—literally zero people. So, when you think about music as a career—first of all, the enjoyment, energy and excitement that I get from being able to do music in-and-of itself is its own greatest reward. So, when you talk about value, or when I think about how you actually provide value to the world as how you make your living, you have to be able to do music on a level that is intrinsically more valuable to the world than it is just for you, who enjoys making the music, right?

GH: Let me just interject, and I'm with you by the way, but this gets into sometimes politically dangerous territory. Is that a sort of libertarian point-of-view, or an entrepreneurial point-of-view, or commercial? You are not saying that there *must* be a commercial element to art, or am I just misreading it completely?

RL: I'm saying that if you want to actually extract value from other people for your art in the form of money or in the form of help as a manager, then you need to be creating art that is giving value to the world, or your story of *why* you're creating art needs to be valuable enough to compel someone to add to that value, right? I don't necessarily think that it's commercial.

In my experience, I've found that people are contributing way beyond just a monetary value. They're actually contributing way beyond just money; they're saying, "hey look, we want to volunteer" or, "see if our company can sponsor you. We want to give you a venue, we want to see if we can contribute something to your music video…"

GH: But Ryan, why? Are you saying they're doing this because they're buying into some sort of greater cause that you're sort of organizing them around? Or are they doing this because there's a quid pro quo where by supporting you they are somehow buying credibility...so if some brand comes and says, "hey we want to support your brand or tour or whatever"—I'm sure they like your music, I started a company to help brands connect with artists, but, in some respects, they are buying the credibility, affiliation, or whatever that you represent. I don't have any problem with that, I think it's good, but I just want to be clear on what you're saying.

RL: That's exactly what I'm saying...someone sent me a video of a TED talk. I'll have to figure out who it is, but they sent me a video of a TED talk about the "why," and that people actually follow people because of this "why."

GH: Right, the purpose. I do a similar talk on that where it's like, businesses have a competitive advantage, and people often say, "it's like x, but with the letter y," with the "y" being cheaper, faster, whatever; and I switch it around and say, "no no no you're like x, but with 'why,'" with the 'why' being a purpose or something that is bigger—or, as you said a moment ago, something which gets you out of bed. People are looking for that. You can become the tip of the spear on that and people will follow.

RL: Yes, absolutely. It's Simon Sinek, by the way.

GH: I know him. He's great.

RL: "How Great Leaders Inspire," it's a TED talk. If you're reading go look it up, it's a great talk. He makes an example about Apple and says "people buy literally anything from Apple," and that's because of the "why." The "why" for Apple is "we're different, we're cool, we're against the status quo," and people buy into that. It's really interesting for me because—and my most recent album is more explicit in the lyrics on this topic—**when you give people a reason to buy in, whatever reason it is, then it becomes more than the music, and you start realizing how valuable you are in somebody's life beyond just the music that you're writing.**

GH: I think that's really important. As the music business moves from a business in which the transactional element was recorded music, in other words, "hey you like me as an artist, great, show that by buying or downloading my album" to something where it's like, "oh you like my music, well you need to support me as an artist," where the transactional element is not recorded music but rather an ongoing and continuous artistic output—then they *really* have to be buying into that "why" of the artist as it relates to their life.

My theory is that great artists and great products—Apple included—are sort of like the magical mirror that Harry Potter stumbles upon, where they reflect back a more idealized version of the person looking into it. So, when people buy Apple computers, it's because feel more creative when they use Apple computers. When people are listening to your music, it's reflecting back something at them that makes them feel better about themselves. All great products do that. That's really the "why." When you do that, people share it because when you find something that makes you feel better about yourself, you share it. I can imagine that's one of the reasons you have been able to spread in the way that you have.

RL: You asked how I got here—my first huge musical success story was with an artist by the name of Cassie. She had 650,000 Myspace friends, and it was one of the first times, maybe the *only* time in music history at that level, where somebody sold as many copies (digital or hard copies) of her record as she had social media followers. 650,000 Myspace friends, 650,000 copies worldwide of her self-titled debut album.

It's just so interesting nowadays when you look at social, or at the huge number of people following you, and you wonder...okay why isn't everyone who is a creator a multi-millionaire? They have all these followers, you know?

What we've found, and what we're finding even more now, is that social engagement is ridiculously low, like unbelievably...and now what I've realized is, how awesome would it be to have as much of a real relationship as possible with the largest percentage of social media followers who would be willing to support you in some way?

So, I went from Cassie selling 650,000 albums, to my first album on Universal selling 180,000, to my second record selling 60,000 albums. Then I went to my record company and asked, "why did we only sell a third of the albums?" And they said "it's because of the music," and all of a sudden, my album got nominated for a Grammy, so I said "well, it's not the music." Then I went back to them and asked, "why wasn't the first line of offense for this new release to email everyone who bought the first album?"

...and for the first time the light went on in my head when they responded and said, "well, we don't know any of those people, we don't have their information...the only way to reach those people again is to go on a major campaign—radio, television, and now social—to try and reach them again and reactivate them." I said that's got to be one of the most backwards, inefficient strategies that I've ever heard of.

GH: Let me interject for a second—this is something I tell artists and clients all the time—everyone is still caught up in the optics of social, but in terms of conversion rates, email still crushes it by a longshot. In other words, you send a tweet out asking your fans to do something, a far lower percentage of people will actually take you up on that than if you sent them an email, is that what you're saying?

RL: Yes, and my startup actually takes it to the next level, which is SMS.

GH: Alright, texting right to them—tell me about it.

RL: At some point about a year ago, I became obsessed with the idea of thanking every person who still cared enough about my music to buy it, just to say, "thank you, thank you so much." As my sales went from 180k to 60k to 20k on an independent release, I said, "oh man, I would love to be able to say thank you to those 20k people," and initially I started out with a MailChimp account. I decided if anyone has bought my album on iTunes or anywhere else, I'll send an email to this email address because I just want to tell you guys "thanks." I thought, "alright this is cool I guess…" And then, while I was at a festival with a bunch of millennials, I asked them, "did you guys get my email?" and they said "we really only check email for work and for school."

GH: Okay this is really good. You're thinking you want to thank them by email, so you send out a bunch of emails via a MailChimp account. You're surrounded by these millennials, or people like 23-24 and under, and you're saying "did you get my email?" and their response is that they only check it for work and school. Am I tracking this right?

RL: Absolutely. So, I said, this is interesting, and thought that maybe I need an app. One of my millennial fans actually suggested an app, and I said okay, but what is my app going to do? He said "it could stream YouTube videos, consolidate all your content into one place." I asked some of the same millennial fans, "how would you like it if I had an app?" and they responded: "Well, we already have enough apps. We already have you on Instagram—we don't need another app." So, I said: "How would you like it if you could just send me a text?" and they were like, "that'd be the coolest thing ever." That's the most retro, analog validation of a relationship with someone.

GH: It's the cassette of relationships.

RL: Yeah! But it's the only way to actually legitimately validate that you have a relationship with someone.

GH: Just to play devil's advocate—and I'm with you and am fascinated by this and want to know how this thing led to your business, but what about Snapchat and other means of communication that millennials seem to embrace whole-heartedly?

RL: The beautiful thing about Snapchat, Instagram, all these other "cool" apps are that you invite them to a pasture, right? **I look at it like you invite all your fans to a pasture, and instead of only the beautiful grass that you have, there's everyone else's grass, and they say "Oh, I can get some of Ryan, some of Chris Brown, get some Rihanna, oh my god everyone is on here I'm gonna follow everyone!" ...and that's really where you end up having incredibly low social engagement.**

GH: Right, because it's not focused. It's not a direct relationship—you end up just scrolling through your Instagram feed, but what about Snapchat? I mean, do you view it in that way? That, to me, seems like more of a direct, one-to-one type of relationship—or am I just looking at that wrong?

RL: Well, it is if you want to send lewd pictures or racy videos. If you have any level of social following, what's going to happen is, you're only going to post on Snapchat in a story. The other kind of challenging piece about Snapchat for me, once again, is that the relationship on Snapchat is my username with some other random username that I have no idea about like "lizlovesryan4579."

GH: Right, too many barriers between the real people. So, this all leads you back to SMS, which you say is sort of an old-school, antiquated technology, but which is essentially you texting people, and you're seeing high conversion with that.

RL: Yes, I'll give you my numbers. I really use Instagram now as a better litmus test of popularity, or relevance if you will, even more so than Twitter, at least in my line of work. I'm at about 160,000 Instagram followers. I was able to convince 36,000 of those people to send me a text message.

GH: That's a pretty high percentage.

RL: Yes, and that all has to do, I believe, with the allure of having that one-to-one relationship. There's no clearer way of saying, "hey I want to be directly connected" than saying "send me a text," so about one-fifth of my Instagram following sent me a text. When people sent a text to my Super Phone, the technology we developed means the phone is smart enough to ask three questions.

GH: And just to be real clear, are you using a specific phone? Did you create a new phone or are you just using an iPhone?

RL: No, it's an application. It's a web application, but it has a native iOS app.

GH: So, it'll work on an Android and on an iOS phone?

RL: Yes, it literally works as long as you have internet access.

GH: So, it's an HTML5, or some kind of responsive-design web app?

RL: Basically, it will ask every single person who sends me an SMS three things. Three interactions that everybody is guaranteed to get as long as they get down my chain. The first one is, "who are you?" which is what anyone would do when you get a text from an unknown number. The first thing you say is, "hey, I got your text and everything, but who is this?" Right? We do this in a way that is a little bit smarter, though. Basically, my phone will hit you back, and actually let's try it out. Anyone who is reading—915-600-6978—shoot me a text. I'm going to predict the future and tell you exactly what you're gonna get from my phone. First, you'll get a text like "Yo! I got your text—click here to add yourself to my phone!"

You'll click a link, and will be redirected to a web form, and when you fill out that web form you get added to the address book on my phone. Then, because I don't sell my music currently on Apple, Amazon, Google Play —for the simple reason that I can't thank people personally for buying my music on those platforms because I don't have their information—my phone will then search my stores, which are Gumroad, Patreon, etc. and see if you've ever bought anything of mine. If you haven't, my phone will send you a link to my latest project. From there, if you actually click the link and buy my latest project, my phone will thank you personally.

GH: So, you've essentially created an API. You've created some sort of machine-learning (for lack of a better word, I'm very tired of that phrase already) where you get people to submit their data through a form. There's an interface layer where people are familiar with it, like texting back and forth. They're filling it out (and I did it by the way...it's a pleasant experience that's really smart in the way that it's like a progress from inception to a reward) and then you gather this information that gets scraped by some sort of machine, API, whatever, and looks for matches within your database from the various APIs that you're grabbing from Pledge or Gumroad. You then identify what, if any, prior connections these people have had with you, and then it automates a message back at them, is that basically right?

RL: It starts to qualify and segment my fan base, so that when someone who is a huge supporter reaches out, I can actually know and differentiate them from someone who is just randomly reaching out.

GH: Perfect, perfect. Let me make sure I've got this. The extent to which someone who does this supports you is determined by various actions they've taken: they've bought a lot of your records, they've tweeted about you, anything you can quantify. Then, you get some sort of notification for super fans, which then compels you to reach out personally, setting a circle in motion where more people are doing more things to get that kind of reward from you.

RL: Absolutely. It's literally a self-fostering, beautiful flywheel for me. Before I had this level of transparency, I didn't know which bands to focus on. I would literally be on Facebook or Twitter, and somebody would say "Hey Ryan I don't like your new song," and as an artist those are the first ones that you want to respond to. Then what happens is the person who says "Ryan I've bought every single album, and I really do love your new song and just wanted to let you know that," and you don't respond to that one, you start to realize, "OK, now I know where to focus my time, energy and attention because there's a value, or a circle of value."

What I've found with this very simple technology is that it allows me to acknowledge and appreciate the people who are *really* supporting me. That's what the release of my latest project was about, it allows me to differentiate people who are saying "you know what, Ryan, you're creating and I'm just with you for the ride."

GH: That goes back to my earlier point that you're now establishing a relationship, which goes beyond the transactional element of the actual song, and more to a relationship with you, the artist. So many things of interest to me here—first of all, this is a classic entrepreneurial move—you had a problem that you faced, you created a technology to solve your own problem, and then, I imagine somewhere along the way, you went, "hey, if this works for me, I bet other people who have the same problem might benefit from this too." Is that right?

RL: Well, that's what I thought, and that's what's so interesting, right? Initially, you know, it was the eureka moment, and I immediately called all my friends like, "oh my gosh guys look at this, this is so amazing, you can know all of your fans and sell directly." I think I was a lot more excited by the amount of money that I was making from very small numbers of people because I had never seen this before in my history as a musician. So, initially my thought process was, oh my goodness look, I sold 20,000 records on an independent deal with Sony Red, and at the end of the 20,000 records I had a royalty balance owed to me of $45,000. Then I thought, I just sold 4,500 copies of my album directly for $10, and I had the same $45,000 and I also have a relationship with those 4,500 people.

That was so powerful to me, so I tried to go talk to my friends, other hip-hop artists, whatever, and they were just like: "#1—I'm still in a deal so that doesn't work for me, and #2—I don't want to be wasting time. I'm already caught up with all my social media and I don't want to be texting and doing all this other stuff," and having people feel like they're obligated to receive responses…it basically just went over everyone's head.

GH: Very important point here for people listening—you have a personality that drove you to do something that others aren't willing to do, that's an entrepreneurial trait. Another thing is, you really didn't have a whole lot to lose. You saw dwindling numbers, going from 150 down to 65 down to 25, and thought "well this is going the wrong way…I can't keep doing this." Then, you go to other artists, and because they don't have the same sort of spirit that you do, they feel they have more risk or just don't have the time. How did you get over that hump?

RL: What's so interesting about this is that I remember sitting down one day and saying, have I lost? Am I just crazy? I was looking around to see who I could speak to about this. I'd read an article about Tristan Walker, so I sent out this tweet telling all my followers to tell Tristan Walker to call me. So, he picks up the phone one day and calls me because he has like 80 tweets at him. He picks up the phone and we talk for thirty minutes. I say, "Hey Tristan, you're in the startup world, you were one of the first employees in FourSquare, the first employees at Twitter, entrepreneur-in-residence at Andresen-Horowitz, you know how important it is as a developer or entrepreneur, how important your very first customers are. You guys are tracking them, you have tools, mix panels, all these amazing tools that help you to know what everyone is doing in your app, etc., and I feel like as musicians we should have that same level of transparency and access to the people who are consuming our products." He says, "Ryan, I think you're absolutely right—you should meet Ben Horowitz." I'm going to be honest with you: I had spent literally my whole entire life just in music—in music circles knowing every who's who of music, writers and everyone, and I had to go and Google...

GH: You hadn't obsessed over venture capitalists? What's wrong with you!

RL: Exactly! That was in the fall, and I had to go on tour, and I didn't get around to getting to Sand Hill Road until January of 2014. I sat in an office with Ben, and explained to him what I was doing. Tristan was like, "this is so cool what he's doing, Ben you have to check this out" and Ben said, "well who put this together?" I told him that I did it myself.

GH: Let me stop you there because this has been nagging at me throughout this whole conversation—did you code it together? Did you cobble together APIs? How did you actually build this thing, the technology?

RL: Codecademy.

GH: Codecademy, right on!

RL: I sat there and figured it out, and when it got beyond what I could tinker with myself I outsourced to a couple of different developers, but you know, we got it done. Ben was just so surprised by this, and so he says "hey, you solved a problem." His response was not much unlike yours. "You solved a problem for yourself that every artist faces. You should go ahead and scale this, and I'd be willing to be part of a seed round." And I said, "well, how much is that?" He said, "ah, maybe about 100 grand," and that was so interesting.

GH: For anyone reading, this guy is a legend, he and his partner Mark Andresen. If they come in (and they don't come in for many things) I mean, you realize now how improbable this story is, but when VCs of that status do, it means that you will have a line of others around the block wanting to throw money at you. People listening shouldn't just think, "oh yeah, I can go down to Sand Hill Road and Ben Horowitz will sit down and write me a check." Anyway, go ahead Ryan.

RL: Basically, I, really early on in my naiveté if you will, was like, "if you're gonna come in to kind of anchor a seed round, and the seed round is only 500 total, I don't need that money, I have that."

GH: So, after he picked his jaw up off the floor, he started adding zeros to that number, I would assume…

RL: This was so interesting right. We didn't close our seed round until May of this year. I initially…

GH: Just to be clear, like two months ago?

RL: Yeah, two months ago. I met with him in January 2014, but it wasn't until two months ago that we actually accepted money from people. It took me a second to even understand what a grave oversight I had done by not accepting his offer. It wasn't Andresen, it wasn't the venture firm—it was him personally. Someone actually had to sit me down and say, "look, Ryan, I just want to give you some context here. There are like ninety Google engineers a week that submit business plans just to get a meeting with this guy. You should take this."

So I said, "okay, yeah. I probably should." And it was great.

Honestly, I have to say on record that Ben and Felicia, his amazing effervescent super-connector of a wife, basically adopted me because they realized I was super wet behind the ears for matters of all things Silicon Valley. They literally just adopted me, and as you would say, super improbable if you will, but at the end of the day I said, "if I'm afforded this opportunity I'm going to do everything I possibly can with it." So, of the usual suspects in terms of filling out this seed round, the first place we went was actually Universal Music Group. They have a venture firm, and they ended up not investing. Then, we went to Troy Carter at Atom Factory and he didn't invest. So we thought, man, if Ben understood it I feel like everyone should just understand it! Literally all of the usual suspects ended up not investing.

GH: Just for context, what was their reason? It just didn't fit their thesis, or what?

RL: If I had to make a guess—even today as we think about it—what's the real scalability of this? Especially if I'm saying that I built a tool for artists to find their top 1,000 fans. They're saying, "alright, what's the business model? Are you gonna be commissioning every fan?"

GH: I wanted to get to that, so is that the issue? What is the business model?

RL: The business model now, because we've been iterating, is

that we're gonna end up taking a piece of every transaction that comes across our platform, like Patreon. We actually weren't involved in payments or transactions at all until about a week ago, and now we've actually worked it out, and that's what we will be doing. Initially, we were just taking a premium on the text messaging. We were kind of charging a bit more than what Twilio was charging us for text messages in return for having that layer of smart technology on top of it.

GH: Oh, believe me, that's micro micro-payments...

RL: Yeah, you'd have to have tens millions of text messages being sent for us to think about anything worthwhile happening from a revenue standpoint. But, in any case, all those people turned us down. Even Nas and Anthony Saleh didn't invest. I'm scratching my head and thinking, "well this is a tool to solve a challenge that the music industry is facing." I remember calling Anthony and asking why they didn't come in, and he said, **"well...artists don't want to be DIY, they want to graduate from being DIY. They want to be signed."**

What was so interesting was that Felicia said "Hey Ry, I really believe in what you've built, and you need to go and tell your story." She actually organized for me to speak at DLD, a big convention in Munich. All the big tech firms and a lot of VCs are there, and Ben was there. I was actually on a panel with Troy Carter. I left DLD, and we'd actually raised another $200,000. We're the only U.S. investment of one of the investors. It's the fund of Kaj

Hed, which is Rovio, which is Angry Birds. So, he has a fund which is just his money out of Sweden called MOOR Cap, and they're actually the largest investor in our seed round at $125,000. They thought that this was just very interesting.

I think in many ways, it just comes down to the passion of the founder. Being this early-stage, we had an MVP, of course, because I'd been using it myself, but we didn't have any revenue. We didn't have a business model. We just had a piece of technology, and I was saying, "look, this piece of technology is changing my life, and is revolutionizing my life, and we believe that it can revolutionize the lives of other artists by raising the veil and providing that level of transparency that even for myself, a semi-veteran in the music industry, has never had." I think there are so many very interesting elements at play, and one of the elements at play here is, how do you teach an old industry that has never had any data, that they need data?

GH: Let me stop you there. This may go to the root of your business model: for this to succeed, do you need that old industry? Do you need Universal or whoever to distribute this across all of their artists? OR, do you go, "you know what, the answer to your question is you don't. Those guys are stuck in the past through fear. Instead, let's go to more of these artists directly." Every day, I see this stark contrast when I go talk to people who are 30 and up about the music business versus when I talk to students who are 30 and below about how you have to be both student and businessperson. Yes, that's hard. Sometimes you need a partner, whatever, but the people who are 30 and below are like, "yeah of course," while the people who are 30 and above are very much stuck in the mindset of, "no, I think I'm gonna make the music and find some label, even though I know the labels are probably gonna screw me." So, who is your target?

RL: My target is really the creator. Basically, I look at the Macklemore story, which is so interesting. I don't have a deep affiliation —I've done a show once with Macklemore at UOP out in Stockton, CA, and I met him backstage. I said, "I love your music," but we've never had the opportunity to sit down and talk. From what I understand, he was grinding it out in Seattle for years and years on end, and he built up an email list of 78,000 or 80,000 people. When you press that button, it said "Hey guys, I really need your support on this record, this is the big hurrah." Enough of those people opened the email, clicked the link, called the radio station, and then boom, he had a 10x, 780,000 records. That's an outlier. **I'm saying, is there a way to accelerate the accumulation of that number of people, or do you even need to accumulate that number of people to have a sustainable career as an artist? This goes back to the blueprint that everyone seems to refer to, which is Kevin Kelley's "1,000 true fans"**

GH: The problem with that, and I love that sort-of meme, is that to get to that thousand true fans, you need at the top of the funnel...I don't know, you tell me, 100,000? 500,000? 1 million people before a thousand people will give you the $8 a

month needed to get to that $100,000 a year based on that model. That's the problem. Maybe what you're introducing will accelerate that, or maybe it will make the funnel more precise so you don't need to have as many going in. The problem with that otherwise really beautiful and aspirational model is that to get that 1,000 people, you need an awful lot at the top of your funnel.

RL: Yes, and I would offer that there is an alternative to that.

GH: That's what I was hoping you'd offer, go ahead.

RL: My alternative is, how many of your Facebook friends can you actually call on the phone? Of the Facebook friends that you can actually call on the phone, how many of them are actually your friends? Then, we start getting into the conversation we were having in the beginning, which is the value. So, the reason why my mom or dad is my number one fan, in my opinion, is because the value that they get from supporting me extends far beyond whether or not they like my music.

GH: I want to talk about this for a second, and this goes back to my Harry Potter theory. They have pride in you and everything, and they're related to you, but they see you and your music and they feel better about themselves. I want to see where this goes, but where I've postulated is that when you have that moment, for whatever it is—you become a vegan, you find yoga, or find God or whatever, **you find something that makes you feel better about yourself on this very emotional level, you tell others about it.**

RL: Yes, you do, and not only do you tell others about it, but you will continue to contribute to that cause. Let's look at the story of one of my interns who wanted to test this out. The first thing that I did with him was a little report card on his social following—450 Twitter followers, 150 Instagram followers, 150 YouTube subscribers, 1,500 friends on Facebook. I asked him, "okay, this is a great case study, how much money have you ever made from music?" He said "zero dollars, in fact I've *lost* money—I gave my last two mixtapes away for free." I asked, "how much did it cost you to make those mixtapes?" He said, "about $2,000 apiece, so I'm down $4,000." Then I asked, "how much money have you ever had in your bank account at one time," and he said $800.

He had come to me because he'd been listening, reading and watching, and everyone says to give your music away for free because people want to try before they buy. Once you've given your music away for free and built up a good following, then you start asking people to support you, and the music is a loss-leader. He was using all these terms, loss-leader, and then you can monetize using shows and merchandise.

GH: Sure, it's a very tired sort-of blueprint which on some levels is hard to argue with, but we just haven't come up with a better alternative...until you're about to explain how you *have*, so go ahead.

RL: I said to him, "okay great, I'm glad you're here, how can I help?" And he said, "well, I've decided to make that step, and I've decided I'm going to monetize my music by doing a concert." I said cool, and asked him to give me the details. He told me, "the Highline Ballroom in New York City has allowed me to have the room on one of their off nights, sell my own tickets, and pay $2,000 for the room." Just for reference the Highline Ballroom has a capacity of 700 people. So, he says, "at $10 a ticket, if I can get 700 people," mind you he has 450 Twitter followers, "at $10 a ticket if I get 700 people I'll have $7,000, and if I pay the $2,000, then I'll have a $5,000 profit." I said "okay from a math perspective, that is profit."

GH: Right, from a simple arithmetic calculation you are correct. Nothing else about that has any bearing to reality whatsoever.

RL: Then I said to him, "okay cool, how many tickets have you moved?" He said seventy, and it was Tuesday and I asked, "when's the concert?" He said "this Friday," and I said, "okay great, what can I do?" And he said, "well that's why I came to you!"

I told him I wouldn't be able to pull a miracle out of my hat here, and he was like, "but can't you tweet my concert to all your fans? You have 500,000 Twitter followers, tweet my concert!" I told him that what I've found, first and foremost, if you look at my Twitter feed my last tweet got maybe 12 retweets, so even though I've got 560,000 people, and that's with me talking about *me*, if I post about you, it may or may not get *any* retweets. **I'd be sur-**

prised if even two or three people buy a ticket at $10 to support me supporting you. So, I said, "look, here's what I'd like for you to do. I'd like for you to give me some time, and let's try out my new hypothesis here." And it wasn't necessarily about the technology, or having a phone number or whatever, it's about a different methodology applied to his challenge.

He said, "okay I'll trust you," and he postponed the concert for 6 weeks. I said, "I want you to refund everybody. We are gonna talk about pricing, and we're gonna talk about real support. My first question is: who is your biggest fan, do you know who your biggest fan is?" He said, "my mom is probably my biggest fan." So I told him to go home and ask his mom—if this concert were a fundraiser for him to make his first real album—how much would she give him for a ticket? He called me the next day and said, "I talked to my mom, and she told me she'd give me $50 for a ticket if it were a fundraiser."

I said, "WOW. First of all, that definitely is your number one fan, and, second of all, put her down for four tickets," so he puts his mom down for four tickets and says, "Ryan, say no more, I absolutely get what you're talking about, I'm taking my $200 and am going to Office Depot to get myself a printer!" I said, "Okay cool...I want you to explain the rationale and logic behind this." He said, "what you're saying is about a relationship, and anyone besides my mom who is willing to give me $50 as a fundraiser for this ticket, I'm going to print out the ticket for them specifically, sign them a personal note, and, if it's within walking distance or train distance, I'm literally going to hand-deliver these tickets."

I told him that's a great idea and he asked, "okay cool, where do I start?" I said, "I'm going to tell you right now how you have an advantage over me on social media." He was like, "okay, now you're really pulling my leg because you have 560,000 Twitter followers and I have 450." I said, "well, according to Twitter I'm able to directly message literally everyone that is following me, but I'm capped at 250 people a day. So, if I started today and never got another follower, it would take me six years to actually direct message each one of them. You have 450 Twitter followers, so you can do it in two days. Same thing with Instagram, same thing with YouTube." Then, that's why I had asked before, "how many of your Facebook friends could you actually call if you needed to?" So, I told him to go directly message his Facebook friends, and to ask his mom, everyone he played basketball with at the community center, college friends, everything, and **literally after over 6 weeks with relentless work, this kid was able to move two hundred people to buy a total of three hundred and seventy-five tickets at $50 apiece. That's $18,750.**

I wasn't able to be there because he had the concert on a Friday while I was overseas, but on Monday I said, "Come by the office," He asked if he could bring his mom, and I told him of course, so he came with his mom, and she couldn't even get through the door without her eyes welling up. She said, "look, before we came here, we went over to TDBank to log in, and when we logged in after we sent the wire over to the Highline Ballroom for $2,000 and paid that out, he had $16,750 in his account. I'm a New York City schoolteacher—it would take me at least six months to earn that much money—much less look at it at one time in the bank. Here I am with my son, who has always wanted to do music and who is always broke from giving his music away, with $16,750 in his account at one time."

That's when I knew, okay, there is a different way to get to that Kevin Kelly 1,000 fans, and it's not about having a huge funnel at the top: it's about worrying about depth over scale.

GH: Okay, wonderful story; inspiring, brilliant, but you can't do that and mentor every artist. How do you make this, and maybe this goes back to why Troy Carter and some of those other people who clearly lack vision turned you down in the funding round, but how do you do this in a way so that it's not just this one dude who you, out of the goodness of your heart or because he's an intern or whatever, mentored? How do you use your technology to make this so that other artists can at least have the hope of that kind of success?

RL: When we raised our seed round, we said, "okay we're gonna raise $500,000 so we can just focus on technology. We'll build an app so that it's easy, and it looks like WhatsApp for your fans or something. If we raise anything over $500k, we're going to put that in a fund to actually test this ideology out as a new-age model for a record label." Hopefully by taking that example that we just gave and being able to do it for an artist that has even more traction, maybe 20,000 or 100,000 Twitter followers, and we get them to profitability and sustainability, we're able to do it as a label. We can then take these best practices and say, "if you want to sign to us you can," but hopefully we can provide an example for what other custodians of art at record labels are supposed to be doing.

Very simply, when we go and talk to them and say, "who is your client," of course the record label should be a client. I had a conversation today with an artist that's on Island Records. He toured with Beyoncé and he literally has 180,000 followers on Instagram, so I said, "How many of those followers can you call? How many records did you sell the last time? How many times have you run into the problem of doing a concert, and then the next day your Twitter followers are saying 'well I didn't even know that you were performing.'" These are all things that, when you sign to a label, as custodians of your art, they should be providing, they should be cognizant of, they should care about.

GH: Yeah, I'm with you. I agree and I've run labels and sort of viewed myself as the custodian of art, and really meant that. I don't know if the labels feel that way or not. My sense and experience is that there needs to be some benefit to them beyond just doing the right thing because labels do *not* have a terribly good track record of doing the right thing for the sake of doing the right thing.

RL: You're absolutely right. So, the benefit, simply put, is efficient marketing.

GH: Okay so you go to the CMO of whatever label and say "you guys need to use this tool." Does that put you in the same boat as other data-related tools out there? I won't mention any names, but there are others out there that people or labels can buy. Is that what you are? Is that the business model?

RL: The business model is that we are going to provide a seamless, frictionless way for people to transact with artists, and we're also going to provide for you, to put it in very crude terms, a reinvention of the fan club. Basically, what we want to say is, if you're going to spend hundreds of thousands of dollars, which is at a very minimum what labels spend to break a new artist, let's see if you can actually get people to convert for life.

GH: Let me ask another question. Is there going to be one platform for labels, and one for unsigned artists? Does everybody have access to this platform, and you're just going to the labels because they're a more effective distribution mechanism, and they can get it out to more artists so that when you take your cut there are more people using it?

RL: Well at the very core of it, it's a communication platform. It's a platform about audience ownership. Probably the best story about this is the story of Bob Johnson and BET. When I got to speak to Bob, and kudos to my former manager Ed Woods who was close with Bob, I had a few chances to sit down and talk with him. What's so interesting about Bob's trajectory is that he's a proclaimed billionaire—he sells his company BET to Viacom. I'm wondering, why is Bob Johnson a billionaire before any record executive or artist? He doesn't rap or sing, he doesn't make albums, and he isn't a record executive. He's doing it on BET, which is music content. I think to myself, **the answer to that is that the real value is in the *audience.* So, either you can monetize your audience directly as an artist, or your influence in your audience is valuable to brands or advertisers, etc.** Bob was getting all this amazing content, Puffy was making $2 million videos...

GH: For free, and making movies, so this guy can run it on BET, and attract eyeballs which he could then sort of commoditize and sell as advertising time, and then eventually sell the whole thing to Viacom.

RL: Absolutely. What's really interesting and not unlike the Bob Johnson story is, here I am with 165,000 Instagram followers, spending time and energy taking the pictures, making sure that there's a guy on tour with me to take pictures, and spending extra money on flights and photo shoots, and on just getting my styling right for when I take the photos.

GH: I wake up with that same emotion every day...

RL: Then what happens is Instagram goes and sells for a billion dollars!

GH: You're going down a path here that's really interesting for me, and I want to weave it back around. I read a post the other day where I made a link, and it's very much a polemic on this, but you've watched this Reddit Revolt, where Reddit users are saying, "screw this, we are not going to spend our time building an audience that Condé Nast, or whoever it is who owns Reddit, can then monetize," and they essentially shut it down.

My thesis was, and I know there are problems with this with respect to consent-decree licenses and everything else, but what if artists said, "you know what, Spotify? You can't have my music anymore because all you're doing is taking my music, bundling it in packaging to try and get subscribers and eventually IPOs are getting acquired, and we get none of that," **and that's sort of what you're saying —that these companies are building their worth off of the contributions of underpaid artists that don't have any equity stake in the thing, and at a certain point artists will say "you know what, I'm not doing this anymore." I think we're a long way from that...**

RL: Yeah, I would say I wish artists even had the power...like, Taylor Swift is on a major.

GH: Sure, Taylor Swift pulls her record down from Spotify because she wants people to buy the download because the margin is so much higher. Neil Young pulls his music off streaming services because, fundamentally he has PONO and he wants people to buy it that way, but I also think that there is a large degree of artists who don't understand that when you sign up through CDBaby, or TuneCore, which is a company that I started, to get your music distributed, you are opting in to this agreement with the Spotifys of the world, so it's not a negotiated license anymore, and you can't pull it off of there!

RL: Absolutely, for the DIY folks that have the ability to pull it from there, but most of the folks have already signed it away, they've already said yes. To look at the silver lining to that, my records are not on Spotify, they're not on any streaming services, but that may be to a level of detriment because I still want my music to be as widely available, and as easily shareable as possible. Since there are so many billions of people on these platforms, it's easy for Mike who works for me to be like "oh look, Ryan's album just dropped, here's a link to share it."

The issue, I think, is very much a deeper systemic issue which holds that it's okay to consume music for free because advertisers are paying for it for free on Spotify. There's no longer any taboo that "hey man, you didn't pay for this music." Well actually, it's legal not to pay for this music and to listen to it for free. Really, I think that what's most interesting about this, and if you look at how I released my last record, it's really just about saying "okay, who's interested in riding with me for the long haul?"

That's the reason why I love a platform like Patreon. It's like, even if you're just a kid in your room, and you can't afford a producer or songwriter, and you're just singing covers because you have a great voice, Patreon gives you a platform and says "hey don't stop doing covers, here's $5!" Honestly, to get the same $5 you would need 5,000 streams.

GH: Oh sure. Or more.

RL: Yeah, so this is really where I think it's going. For me, I think that the discovery helps with that top-of-the-funnel conversation we were having. Eventually, my last two albums will go up on Spotify, but it won't be on Spotify so that I can make money from streams—it'll strictly be for discovery and shareability, if that's a word. Basically, what I'm interested in, and this is what I talked to my friend about today, is using the marketing dollars to see whether or not you can get people to subscribe to your creativity, or your ability to create for as long as possible.

When I look at Amanda Palmer's Patreon page, I think she really has it right. She's saying, "look, I'm an artist. It's not about one album or me performing that album, it's about me creating on a consistent basis because this is what I've chosen to do as my career pathway."

GH: We keep going back to that thread of "support me, the artist, in my ongoing output rather than a particular song or piece of work." To try and tie a little bit of a bow around this, you have a product that is working. You're now talking to others. At the end of the day, what problem are you really trying to solve? Because I'm still a bit unclear on it.

RL: The problem, or the challenge that I'm trying to solve for, simply put, is how does the artist actually own the audience that they've worked so hard to amass?

GH: Let me stop you right there, and I hate to interject right in the middle of your main idea, but I can't help myself. If I'm a label, who actually owns that audience if they use your tool? The label or the artist?

RL: For us, it would have to be a joint ownership. If I issued you a phone number and you said, "hey this is my new phone number for anyone who is interested in having a little bit deeper understanding of my writing, and eventually I'm going to write up an autobiography of all my findings, here's my number." The way that our terms of services are, I, Ryan Leslie, even though I own the platform, can't decide "hey my new album is coming out now let me just hit all of George's fans"—unless there is a consent there. I could say, "hey George, can you hit all the folks who sent out a text with my album cover" and you say, "hey Ryan, cool I'd love to do that." There's a compliance there, or a a willingness to co-promote, if you will.

GH: I guess that makes sense. I just remember, back in the stone age when websites were sort-of a new thing, and I was running the label, most artists didn't know how to build a website. We'd say, "look, we'll build the website for you, we'll host it for you, and collect the email addresses, and oh by the way, we own it." That was not constructive, or as you say being a steward of the art or whatever, it was just sort of a grab.

RL: So, for us it's really just about, how do you own your audience? If Instagram shuts down tomorrow, how are you going to get your message to the tens of thousands of people who follow you? If Twitter shuts down tomorrow, and we ran into this sort of with Cassie, 650,000 Myspace followers, boom, Myspace becomes a graveyard and all of that equity is suddenly gone. How awesome would it have been if she had 650,000 mobile numbers and email addresses? Incredible. And then, above and beyond the ownership of the audience, which I think is the root of the challenge, how do you differentiate between those who are willing to support and those who are just passively following? How do you actually differentiate between those people? Because, a little bit of sugar and spice on the ones who *really* want to support you will lead to even greater relationships, greater engagement, and will lead you to recognize the people who will follow you around the world, like the people who followed Jimmy Buffet around the world!

That's what it is about, and that's what we're solving for, very plain and simple. One: own the audience. Two: be able to qualify, differentiate and segment between the folks that are willing to pony up and support in some way, and that can be in any way. You can say, "look, these are my most evangelical fans on Twitter, these are my most supportive fans in terms of dollars spent, these are my most influential fans because they're journalists." Literally you can login to my tool and type in "journalist," or "fashion," or "tech," and all of the people who fall in that category, you'll be able to segment them and say "okay wow, let me go through all of the people who are in PR."

GH: I like that, and that gets at something I was talking to Andy Weissman, a guy who I think we both know about. He's got a sort of a, as he calls it, "Nirvana State for the Blockchain:" and a sort of music registry where you would list the data in a public record, and then machines could scrape it, and you would list rules that you could have around your music. You could say, "yes, I'll allow this to be streamed, I'll allow derivatives of it," and you're doing a similar thing. You'll eventually have to open up the API, I suppose, so people can select it, but you are at least creating this database that could then be utilized.

RL: Yes, absolutely, and that's really what we want to do. The data eventually becomes a private registry of every music consumer or every artist that's in our ecosystem. That's really beautiful because then I can see how many fans of my friend Nipsey Hussle are also fans of mine? How many fans of 50 Cent are also fans of mine? If I notice the overlap is only like 10%, maybe I could convince 50 to hit all of his fans and introduce them to me, because they obviously don't know about me.

GH: Exactly, and this expands, as I'm sure Ben Horowitz was saying, to other forms of art. There's no axiomatic reason that this has to just be music. I just started a company, and I sent you the link,

Artgasm, which is a subscription model for fine artists. The reason that this type of thing is succeeding is because, just by virtue of the price-point and everything else, you are going to get a very direct, personalized relationship with this artist that you love. That's really what you're buying. In the fine art world, in some respects, that's a little bit easier to understand because you have this tangible good—whereas in the music business, and this is why vinyl is making a comeback. It's all digital—you don't have a thing. So, I guess your model could work for other art forms too.

RL: The last thing I'll leave you with is, for Patreon and for Drip - we actually just met the guys at Drip, and they introduced me to Andy. For those models, what we found is that a direct invitation to support that comes *from the artist*, nine times out of ten, leads to a 50% conversion. Of the 36,000 people who sent me a text, 33,000 opted to add their information to my phone, and about 15,500 ended up buying or spending some type of money with me. The reason why it's 50%, and I don't know if it scales...but in any case, what's interesting is that if I could just ask you "hey George, can I borrow $10?" It's going to be 50/50. Somebody's getting sold. Either you're going to give me $10, or you're going to sell me on a reason why I can't have your $10. So basically, for Artgasm, for Drip, for Patreon—imagine if people can ask a few questions before they even subscribe voluntarily.

GH: It's about context.

RL: Yeah, and it leads to a direct ask, albeit the direct ask is

driven by some technological advancement. The ask is still in my voice, and it's still what I would ask if I had the time to respond to everyone personally. So that's our vibe, man.

GH: It's a good vibe, and it's wildly exciting to me because it's a really tangible tool for connecting artists with their fans or customers in a meaningful way that has some good conversion rates using this hodge-podge of interesting new technologies that can grow and flow with the different changes. Even though it's reliant on SMS, which some people might say is outdated. Watch a bunch of 16-year olds with their phones and see what they're doing—they're just texting back and forth like crazy. So, congratulations to you, and I can't thank you enough for taking a long part of your evening to talk with me tonight. It's really a pleasure to talk to you, congratulations on everything.

RL: Yeah, we gotta stay in touch man, and I just really appreciate you reaching out. For anyone that's reading, you probably have gone through my SMS chain, so you've gotten the responses and everything. If you do get my album, you'll get a thank you from me. When you write me after that, you're in a special box because I know who you are and you've given me some support. As it stands right now, I'm currently managing, and if anyone from WhatsApp is listening or reading, if I'm looking at my phone right now, I'm currently managing over 20,000 conversations on WhatsApp, and 14,457 of them are not actually responded to because they won't open their API and allow me to do this. And so, eventually, I don't think it's SMS per sé, but I do think it's messaging. **Whether it's Telegram, or WhatsApp, or Line or WeChat or Facebook messenger, someone please open the API so that my fans can communicate with me for free instead of paying international SMS fees, and so that I can actually build this response chain and make sure that everyone who reaches out to me gets a response.**

GH: Right on, it's a call-to-action and I see no reason why they wouldn't do it. Thanks again for this, Ryan, it's very inspirational and I appreciate it.

RL: You got it man, and for anyone who wants to stay in touch you have my number, 915-600-6978. I'm also on all of the more…how should I say...standard social media stuff, Twitter, Instagram, it's always Ryan Leslie, but George thank you so much for the time and for having me.

PART IV

INTERVIEWS WITH VENTURE CAPITALISTS

Union Square Ventures' Andy Weissman On the Blockchain And the Music Rights 'Nirvana State'

Blockchain As the Source-DNA For Content Attribution: A Conversation with Bill Tai - Part 1

Bill Tai Interview Part 2: "The Structural Unlocking of Spirits: Artists as Entrepreneurs"

UNION SQUARE VENTURES' ANDY WEISSMAN ON THE BLOCKCHAIN AND THE MUSIC RIGHTS 'NIRVANA STATE'

Jul 19, 2015

I'm not sure what your stereotypical view of a venture capitalist is, but it's likely *not* someone who quotes from Grant Hart and Ken Kesey on his blog pieces that have titles like, "No-Stack Startups" or "The Chaos Theory of Startups."

I don't recall exactly how Andy Weissman—who is a Partner at Union Square Ventures—and I first got to know each other, but likely we bonded over music and books, and...maybe...we talked about entrepreneurship/VC too.

I always know I'm onto something when I post an article and Andy chimes in on Twitter, as he did regarding my recent interview with Zoe Keating about her take on the Blockchain Summit and her thoughts generally on crypto as it relates to artists.

I'm enjoying my journey down the rabbit hole of Crypto, and am happy that I'm finding a lot of fellow travelers—like Imogen Heap, who presents a fascinating vision for her usage of the Blockchain to create a whole new system for music, which she calls Mycelia—who are raising the level of discourse on this confusing topic.

I took Mr. Weissman's tweet as an invitation to follow up with him in order to get his thoughts on the Blockchain.

I'm glad I did. In the interview below, Mr. Weissman concisely lays out a framework for what he calls the "Nirvana State" for how we might apply the Blockchain to the music business.

Below is a transcript of my email interview with Mr. Weissman. It has been lightly edited for clarity and grammar. (Bonus points to anyone who—*without googling it*—can identify the band Mr. Weissman quotes at the end of the interview.)

George Howard: After your tweet, I reached out, and asked you to elaborate on your 140 characters. You quickly responded with one of the more succinct—as you call it— "Nirvana States" for the applicability of the Blockchain. I'm going to excerpt it here:

- "Assume no change in copyright laws in the US.
- To afford yourself of those protections, you must 'register' your copy on the Blockchain. In that way, the 'rights' will be publicly listed. As those rights may be transferred, the chain of ownership will as well.
- One benefit here could be that one could also stamp your own rules on that copy. Programmatically, we would see what you desire as to that piece of media and how it may be used. These of course could change over time, as you desire.
- This would then be a decentralized registry, but even more as the rules would be machine-readable. This could enable apps and services to be built on top of them.
- This could achieve the end state of being the nirvana music API."

So, I think I get you up through about halfway in point four. You're saying, I believe, that artists (or any holder of a copyright) would register that work on the Blockchain, and add in limitations ("rules") around how others may or may not interact (create derivatives, reproduce, etc.) with the work.

But, from there, it gets hazy. Can you clarify the idea of building apps and services on top of them, and explain how this results in the "nirvana music API?"

Andy Weissman: Once the rights are publicly listed in this way—on the Blockchain—anyone would be able to see them. More so, they would be machine-readable. And, a person—or a machine—could see the rules the artist expresses for that piece of media. Ian Rogers expressed it this way over 3 years ago pre-Blockchain consciousness:

"You, the content owner, could set the rules and the prices. Which tracks are available for free download? Available for streaming? How long a streaming sample allowed? High definition? At what price points? The market could decide if the price you're asking is fair: 'My service only supports downloads with a wholesale price of $0.70.' 'My service is only interested in free downloads.' 'My service is only interested in content which is available for subscription streaming.'"

So, the idea could be that a machine could read those rules—and then build a music service on top of that. No more interminable contract negotiations over these.

GH: As a venture capitalist, part of your job is to look outward to a more ideal future, and to time your investments at or just before the intersection of market demand and technological development. Let me play devil's advocate here for a second; what if the market does not demand what Crypto offers in any meaningful way, and the technology—be it the registry you reference, etc.—does not become a reality? I hope I'm wrong, and that you'll disabuse me of these fears.

AW: Maybe you are wrong, maybe you are right. We have the advantage of a business model that provides us the opportunity to invest in companies that are trying to create a world we would like to exist.

Sometimes we are right about that, sometimes not—**but, an analogy: mobile apps didn't exist before 2007 or 2008. Look how much has changed in just those few short years.**

"Once in awhile you get shown the light in the strangest of places if you look at it right."

BLOCKCHAIN AS THE SOURCE-DNA FOR CONTENT ATTRIBUTION: A CONVERSATION WITH BILL TAI - PART 1

Aug 27, 2015

Bill Tai is a truly inspiring person. It's not so much his success as a VC—though, that is pretty off the charts—but, more, the fact that even with this success, Mr. Tai continues to keep pushing; expanding out beyond traditional Venture-based activities (if there is such a thing), into endeavors that are as focused on impact as they are profit.

Along with Susi Mai, Mr. Tai created MaiTai Global, which holds events across the country that focus not only on advancing and elevating the discourse on relevant topics, but also on philanthropy. [Disclosure: I will be participating in the upcoming MaiTai event on the Music Industry.]

My conversation with Mr. Tai was wide-ranging, and below are excerpts related to Bitcoin and Blockchain, and, specifically, **how Blockchain technology could help solve what I believe to be the fundamental issue for today's creator—be they a musician, writer, visual artist, etc.—attribution.**

In my exploration of Blockchain, I am very encouraged by the technology's ability to better track and transact efficiently—*once content has been registered on the ledger.*

What I am deeply uncertain of/concerned by is the fact that—to date— neither Blockchain/Bitcoin technology nor

anything else is remedying the problem of attribution for what is being entered on the ledger. That is, if someone puts something on the distributed ledger that they don't have the rights to, the Blockchain tech will only exacerbate problems around rights and identity, rather than fix them.

Watch this space for future excerpts of my conversation with the fantastic Bill Tai; including his thoughts on the recent Bitcoin fork. As stated, below is an excerpt of a longer conversation, and so you're joining us somewhere in the middle of our talk (it has been lightly edited for content and clarity):

George Howard: So, this does lead me, I guess, in a strange way to Crypto or Blockchain. Insofar as, data has to be track-able from some sort of source, right? I've been writing about this for a few months, and it's been amazing to watch the energy in the space.

Zoë Keating was one of the first people I talked to about Blockchain technology and its relationship to the arts, and she did a great piece with me. I also talked to people like Imogen Heap, and I keep going down this rabbit hole—not only because I want to talk to people who are smarter than I am and get insight, but because it has opened up for me this broad, expansive potentiality. I'm going to use a phrase here that I know is wrong, but Blockchain tech is almost like a shot at replacing the internet. It's almost a shot for us to do it again—**and to do so thinking about things like attribution.**

I would love to hear your thoughts on this. I know you've funded a company called BitFury, so this is something that's very much on your mind. Give me your thoughts on Blockchain tech and how it relates back to data.

Bill Tai: Valery Vavilov founded BitFury. It's one of the bigger companies in the space of running infrastructure around the world that processes Bitcoin and Blockchain.

To go back to the big picture of what you said of a "chance to do it again" —basically, what I see is that the internet allowed us to packetize information and make it fluid and accessible everywhere. What Cryptocurrency does is it packetizes values; it allows us to transmit them in a mobile, liquid way anywhere.

GH: Make a distinction for me. That's incredibly insightful—make the distinction for me between "packetizing information" and "packetizing value."

BT: So, to the extent that you can take little tiny pieces of information—if you look at the alphanumeric, you know, the alphabet that we all use—if you could express letters and numbers in 1's and 0's going across air, or wires, you could convey words, sentences, and thought, express ideas, and allow the information to flow anywhere. What something like Cryptocurrency does is, instead of using letters or numbers, it basically takes tiny amounts of value that can be aggregated in any amount and sent anywhere any time—like you could send an email.

GH: Right.

BT: So, it's revolutionary in that it totally reduces friction and overhead related to instant payment. You know, if somebody does good work on something, and you want to reward them with some value, it's instantaneous.

GH: So, it's not just about the reduction of transaction costs. Obviously, that's incredibly important, but it's also that, as you said, "Somebody does good work," and you want to compensate them, give them some value.

BT: I'm with you.

GH: For me, one of the key things—something I'm wrestling with and hope you'll shine some light on—is that it's also that sort of... what's the word? "Credit" is the wrong word, but it's "validation."

BT: Tipping—there's a tipping thing that's...

GH: Well, there is that, but let me give you a personal example: so, I write an article the other day for Forbes, and it's about how Blockchain could allow us to sort of reinvent the internet, right?

And then two days later, 400 people send me a link to some other article and say, "George, this sounds an awful lot like your article."

But the author didn't reference back to my articles. They did reference Imogen Heap, and I thought, "Oh okay, they're going to quote back to the 4,000 words that I wrote on Imo-

gen in my article on her." They didn't. There's no plausible way that they didn't know my articles existed. They *chose* not to give me attribution, and that's okay. I guess.

But then, there were these sort of SEO blogs, right, and they had taken my article and re-blogged it all over the place with no attribution; took my byline away, all those types of things.

BT: Right.

GH: And so, how does Blockchain tech remedy this?

BT: There is a way to fix that. The technology exists, but the implementation is not there yet. Blockchain is an identity management system.

GH: Yes.

BT: When we talk about how value can be transmitted in a liquid way, the only way it can be transmitted is if the underlying technology knows and identifies the sender and the recipient—if it knows who they are and also uniquely identifies a piece of content or value that goes from Point A to Point B. If it records it and knows it, it's indelible. It's written down and copied—kind of like it's imprinted in a ledger. It's there permanently.

GH: But if I put something up onto the ledger that I don't have the initial rights for, how does that—and I've heard different answers to this question—then get disproven?

What's to keep me from putting stuff on the ledger that I don't have the rights to and claiming it as mine?

BT: Right, so this is why I said the functioning of technology is there, but the implementation is not what it should be. Whatever the standard should be has not arrived yet.

GH: Got it, okay.

BT: At the Necker Blockchain Summit, we broke up into teams of seven or eight people and asked the entire group, in their teams, to come up with things that could be implemented on the Blockchain that could be game-changing. Oliver Luckett, a social media expert, had the idea of a social media genealogy system.

GH: Okay.

BT: As you're saying about the articles that you write—say some kid posts a really cool video on YouTube, and then somebody downloads it and reposts it on a blog that they may have built up into a little media site. They get 3 million views and lots of ad dollars, and that kid gets nothing.

GH: You got it. That's the music business, by the way, that you've just described. But go ahead.

BT: **What if, when a piece of content is originated as a piece of currency would be originated, it gets listed on the Blockchain with the identity of the content and the identity of the person tied together? And every time it moves—like in the Bitcoin case, every time somebody repaid me and I took a piece out of it and paid you—it would record it as a transaction, but it would know where the source was.** So it's a way to almost look at the genealogy, like you can look up the ancestry of any piece of content from where it was originally created.

GH: So the premise there would be—to use your example—the kid puts up something that she didn't have the rights to or didn't create or whatever, by downloading it the first time. If that first creator had put it up, there'd be a ledger that says, "Hey, wait a second. This wasn't yours." So you've created a derivative work, and now we can track down the "genesis block" or what have you.

BT: Exactly, exactly. Right.

GH: I get that, but I'm not sure. The other thought is more like Xanadu Project-type stuff where you get credibility over time and by your association. **I've written a hundred articles for Forbes on this thing—now I've got a sort of credibility level, and it's unlikely that I'm going to rip somebody off. You almost build a currency based on reputation and legacy. Maybe that works, I don't know.**

BT: That could work too, reputation engine on top of it.

GH: Exactly, but this is so, so unbelievably fundamental to the music business when we talk about how Blockchain may help rights holders. I mean, if you don't have that original, unfettered copyright, and you sign up on some registry, all you're doing is exacerbating the problem at that point.

BT: Right. Yeah, the technology does have the potential. What I think needs to exist is what is being built now from a technology perspective, which is a super scalable, very low-cost infrastructure.

GH: Right.

BT: So you can track everything. I think that if the currency movement really takes hold and takes off, then there's lots and lots of infrastructure that's being subsidized by the currency movement, which other things can be built upon.

Then you can run stuff on top of it for some low nominal fee to stimulate usage because it has to be very pervasive, which it can be, though it has to be low cost. Those two elements do exist, and one of the things I would love to see BitFury do is build this out.

We have this very cool project to put Bitcoin miners in light bulbs and kind of give them away or sell them at low cost and stimulate usage. Each one of those is an effort to get the gigantic nodes out there that could be running a Blockchain under them.

Therefore, there is no one company out there that has to bear the burden of processing all the information out there on the web, and people could develop applications. They just access it. They hold it. And they let the market forces rule, and things that are needed win out.

GH: Right, right. We need that stimulation. And again, people get "pissed" at me when I say this, but I always say "Bitcoin is to the Blockchain as porn was to the internet." I know those are tethered together, but because of the economic imperatives there, and the potential for riches and everything else, Bitcoin is going to drag other use cases connected to the Blockchain behind it. I think.

BT: I agree.

BILL TAI INTERVIEW PART 2: "THE STRUCTURAL UNLOCKING OF SPIRITS: ARTISTS AS ENTREPRENEURS"

September 22, 2015

In the first part of my discussion with the wildly successful and deeply conscious VC, Bill Tai, we discussed how Blockchain technology could aid in the ascribing of proper attribution to creators. Certainly this is a fundamental problem, as – absent some type of verification system—we are faced with a "garbage in" problem that the Blockchain, with its distributed ledger, will only exacerbate.

The other issue for creators, of course, is related to discovery. Assuming that one's work is accurately recorded on the ledger, how do we possibly expect others to *find* this work amidst the countless others?

This problem of discovery has bedeviled us since long before the internet. However, whether it was via the The Long Tail—crowd-sourced "wisdom"—or algorithms, technology has held out the promise of better recommendations and discovery.

Perhaps there are not enough "heads" to pull those who are further down the demand curve up the tail to greater prominence; perhaps the crowd has no wisdom; perhaps the algorithms don't work. Or, perhaps, as I've posited: **we simply don't want to discover new things nearly as much as the media/pundits/entrepreneurs would have us believe.**

The truth, as it usually does, likely lies somewhere in the middle. Sometimes—through technology or via old-school word of mouth—we do discover something that delights us, and we feel that surge of the joy of the new.

In this second part of my discussion with Mr. Tai, we talk about his brilliant presentation, "Internet Waves of Growth and Investment." An important component of this thesis is that we are now at the "Wave" where we start adding structure to heretofore "unstructured data."

This Wave should finally move us past the largely worthless "curation," and begin helping us to better draw inferences across ostensibly disparate tranches of "unstructured data."

There are implications of this expand into virtually every facet of our lives—health to music to thermostats—and Mr. Tai and I discuss them all. The conversation has been lightly edited for grammar and clarity, but otherwise is transcribed verbatim from our conversation.

George Howard: Quoting the great Hugh MacLeod, I have long held that "all artists are entrepreneurs, and all great entrepreneurs are artists." You have worked with thousands of entrepreneurs, mentored them and nurtured them. In this era, when musicians are increasingly forced to be entrepreneurs, or act like they're little start-ups or what have you—what guidance might you offer?

Bill Tai: Well, I think we are in an era when it just pays to try. I think the frame of reference is that people don't know how lucky they are today.

If you think about what it was like to become a band or to become a performing artist thirty or forty years ago, you really were at the mercy of the corporations in a way that controlled production and distribution. Because the capital intensity of printing vinyl records and shipping them out in...

GH: ...Before you event got to that point, to get to the studio you had to trade away your assets. You had to trade away your sound recordings just to properly go into the studio.

BT: Yes, exactly. I think the capital intensity that occurred around every form of media production and distribution—whether it is settling for the infrastructure of printing newspapers or transponders or what have you, or the distribution over radio for records—put the artist in the position where they were a cog in the gigantic system.

Now with a laptop or a smartphone, you have your own entry point, control over the origination, some access to distribution, and the ability to potentially break out. I am fascinated at the moment at the rise of the "Vine artists."

GH: Yeah, yeah. There could be copyright issues, but, I hear you. Go ahead.

BT: I don't know if I should call them Vine artists, but it is sort of a different form of art. You see these kids do seemingly weird routines in fifteen seconds that get ten million views on Vine. They aren't really songs, but they are entertaining.

I think we are in a world where it just pays to try innovations. It's easier to fail, if you try, and if you fail you learn. Society has never been more geared to rewarding just the attempt. It is a very spiritually unlocking thing to be able to be free to try.

Think about what the image of corporate America was like in the fifties: you know, with guys in suits on Madison Avenue and gigantic companies where you would work for IBM, or the "salaryman" in Japan. Now you can make your own career as an entrepreneur or artist.

You are right: every artist is an entrepreneur and every entrepreneur is an artist. And that's wonderful.

GH: Agreed, but with these lower barriers of entry and a culture of trying, there are challenges. Essentially, the barriers come down; everyone piles in, and it's harder and harder to stand out.

I'd like to talk about that as it relates to one of your presentations that I really love, "The Next Big Wave of Internet Investments." In it you go through the four waves which lead us to the fifth wave, which is "big data."

At its core, all of this new content being created by artists is data, and our challenge is really organizing and collectively storing the data. Health and genomes—those types of things. Did you want to add anything to that? Am I off-base there, or is that an accurate description?

BT: No, but I think it's probably useful for the audience to understand what you are referencing.

When I started in this business, I originally designed semiconductor chips. It wasn't so institutional at the time, but there was a wave of companies in the late seventies through the mid-eighties whose primary value proposition was the integration of technology into transistors. So, they were replacing vacuum tubes so that you could build stuff that burned less power and was portable. That was kind of wave one.

Then there was the second wave, which was the assembly of those—like Lego blocks.

GH: Generally Dell and those types of companies.

BT: Yes, yes. The computer systems, subsystems, communication systems—that was a very investable wave through the 90's. All those little boxes got stitched together, which was the digitization of the communications infrastructure.

So, the formation of ISP's and co-location and hosting companies—the roots of Amazon's cloud business—that was a third big wave.

Then there was a fourth wave: once technology could come to users through a browser, like water coming out of a faucet or electricity coming out of an outlet. They were changing those types of companies to a user interface.

GH: Right.

BT: Many of the companies you see on your apps, they are really just user interfaces to data coming off of the cloud, and it's the way that you move and massage and handle the data that creates a ton of value.

GH: Sure.

BT: I think because the companies were in their respective categories in that way, the techniques that were applied to allow those companies to win were largely based around some technologies that people may or may not have heard of—like Hadoop—and have created this wave of companies that are known for big data.

I think that type of power wasn't really economical before because the cost of storage was too high and the ability to have insight was just not possible. But now you can manage and process trillions and trillions of pieces of information every day.

In the "brick and mortar" world, a company like Walmart kicked ass because they were really a physical user interface to a pile of data.

GH: Right, right.

BT: They know what moves at the endpoints better than companies like JC Penney, which had lots of inventory problems, did. Sears and JC Penney went bankrupt, or near bankrupt, because they didn't handle efficiently what was in their system.

GH: So, it's like you are saying that Walmart almost had a better CRM. The store was the UI and the people were the "bits and bytes" that went through, and Walmart was able to extract more information out of that than a Sears or whomever that just did not analyze the behavior as efficiently. It's really interesting.

BT: Yeah. They are hugely efficient because every time you check something out at the register at Walmart, they know down to an item and a skew where the flow was. You could almost look at products in that system like "bits" coming over the internet.

GH: Yeah. That's what I was trying to get at. That's great.

BT: And that is being applied everywhere. So now you take that knowledge framework and you can apply it to so many things that people refer to as "unstructured data."

Well, if you think about the information that is contained at a group level across every single power meter hanging off of every home—if you could watch it from the position of a conductor of an orchestra looking at the flow of things and know how to mediate and moderate demand, and you are more effective at pricing—you are more effective at building your infrastructure.

GH: Is that Google's gambit with Nest?

BT: I think it is. Absolutely yes, and that is happening more and more as easy-to-use infrastructure to handle massive amounts of data becomes readily available from companies like Treasure Data. Treasure Data is a four-year old company that has scaled to ingest 3 trillion rows of data per day from customers like Toyota Motors. In that particular use case, the company is monitoring all of the engine data coming off a few percent of Toyota's hybrid automobiles throughout the day to better understand engine performance across time of day and traffic conditions.

They can tell how cars are being utilized at a global level, what the engine performance looks like during various times of day, rush hours and not, and how people are using the cars. They are using this data to drive better efficiency in their design of engines going forward.

GH: I love the promise of this. The thing that I keep waiting for and almost have to build myself—or maybe you will—is a dashboard for me.

I got sick, but I got better through becoming largely vegan and being very, very careful of what I put into my body. And I can envision the interface, right. I can see the interface that I want.

I want levels where I wake up in the morning and it says, "Here is where your blood sugar is, etc." And then when you eat or ingest what you are going to ingest, you should see those levels rise and fall in relation to activity and everything else. Why is that so hard? How can we not be closer to something like that where I can say, "I really need to go eat something that has more X, Y, and Z, in it?"

BT: It's coming. We are headed there for sure. I think Samsung has a pretty good initiative in that area. We are a little ways away from it, but there is a gentleman who is the President of Samsung's innovation—I forget what they exactly call it—who runs a big unit and is in charge of "strategy and innovation," and they launched "wearable."

It looks like a watch, but it measures all kinds of things in our blood without being invasive. It's not a needle, but they are basically monitoring flow by shining a number of different frequencies of light through different LED's into your skin. Ultimately, they want to measure more than just your heart beat—also blood sugar levels and all types of good things.

GH: That is so interesting to me. I love the idea of looking at these concepts and applying them to different things. One of the things that I have taken some hits (as well as some nice comments) for is that I said that our algorithms or what have you for recommending things like "new music" are terrible.

My thesis is: "So, I like The Who, but please don't tell me that I will like the Rolling Stones." That's one degree of separation. You need to go out further than that.

But this conversation really gets my mind thinking: it is less about recommending based on "music to music," and more about "music to other things." And that to me seems the promise of data that is much broader than these sort of arbitrarily constructed verticals that we keep seeing.

BT: That's exactly right. A lot of the inference gained in each task was based on limited data. And now the technology exists around particularly this infrastructure technology called Hadoop where you can take disparate heterogeneous data sets, and combine them into one table to see what correlation there might be across what's called "unstructured data."

GH: So, Bill, you have been so generous with your time, and I can't thank you enough. I've loved this conversation. **Lots of topics covered, but the through-line seems to be this idea of using technology to balance or combine seemingly disparate parts. That's entrepreneurship, right?**

My image for the successful entrepreneur everyone should aspire to be is you. I think I got this image from your Facebook photos, but I have this image of you in your cowboy hat, ready to kite surf and solve deep and profound problems that impact society in a better way. I appreciate this very much, thank you very much for talking to me today.

BT: Well thank you, and I hope that I can have some impact and inspire some people to have fun and do good while they are having fun.

PART V

CONVERSATIONS WITH CEOS, FOUNDERS AND ARTIST MANAGERS

CASH Music Helps Run the Jewels and Others Achieve Success by Disintermediating the Music Business

Benji Rogers' .bc Codec: A Fair Trade Approach to Music and Virtual Reality Using the Blockchain

Benji Rogers Gets Specific About the .bc Codec: A Fair Trade Music and VR Solution Using Blockchain

Mediachain Facilitates Automatic Attribution Using Blockchain And Machine Learning

PRS For Music CEO, Robert Ashcroft, Discusses Challenges and Innovations in Music Collection

CASH MUSIC HELPS RUN THE JEWELS AND OTHERS ACHIEVE SUCCESS BY DISINTERMEDIATING THE MUSIC BUSINESS

Aug 26, 2015

Jesse Von Doom is on a mission. The particular windmill that Mr. Von Doom tilts towards—via his organization, CASH Music—is helping artists create sustainable careers without relying on labels or other "intermediaries." Unlike others, Mr. Von Doom comes at this approach in a truly evolved manner. For instance, Mr. Von Doom made a statement during our wide-ranging and free-wheeling conversation that has literally kept me awake at night since we spoke last week:

> "You can go after money, credit, or change."

Are these mutually exclusive? Is it analogous to the "Project Management Triangle" of: "Choose two: You can have it fast, cheap, or good?"

While I and others ponder these questions, Mr. Von Doom doesn't bother with such trivialities, and instead focuses squarely on "Change."

To this end, for roughly the past eight years, Mr. Doom has been the co-executive director, along with Maggie Vail, of CASH Music. [Disclosure, I was one of the original CASH board members many moons ago, but for the past years have limited my involvement to simply being a fan and informal advocate.]

CASH Music—like so many entrepreneurial enterprises—originated as a solution to a problem that, at the time, seemed only relevant to a specific few people. Specifically, Kristin Hersh, her manager, Billy O'Connell, and Donita Sparks of L7 and her manager, Robert Fagan, **determined that they would be far better off devising a model in which their fans were able to directly contribute to sustaining their artistic output than they would going the traditional label route. Through solving this problem for themselves, it became clear that the solution they originally devised for their own needs, could also benefit others, and, CASH was born.**

As familiar as the concept of connecting directly to fans sounds now, back in 2007, this was revolutionary. I genuinely don't believe that Ms. Hersh/Mr. O'Connell nor Ms. Sparks/Mr. Fagan get the credit they deserve for "Kickstarting" the whole "Patreon-age" system of fans "Pledge[ing]" in order to support Indie[gogo] artists without having to rely on labels or other systems that too often are full of [top]spin.

But, again, as Mr. Von Doom says: "Money, credit, or change."

Over the years, CASH has certainly brought forth change by enabling artists to better and more-efficiently connect with their fans. To date, roughly 7,500 artists have created CASH accounts, and the embeds of CASH tools utilized by these artists have been seen by 3.6 million people.

Beyond the "money, credit, change" dynamic, what strikes me the most about what CASH is doing is the long-term accumulation of knowledge about fan/artist relationships.

The music business has for too long been an *ad hoc* enterprise, (wrongly) believing that nothing is to be gained by the experience of others. To my mind, beyond the tools, CASH's true value is accumulated knowledge. CASH is empirically discovering: What works? Why? When? What's verifiable and repeatable? What falls under the dreaded "correlation without causation"/*post hoc ergo propter hoc*

The good news is, true to its Open Source ethos, CASH will not only move forward by providing the tools, but also its learnings. The two together—tools and knowledge—of course, are what the industry truly needs, and this combination explains why newer artists like The Joy Formidable, Zola Jesus, as well as artists/labels who have seen the other alternatives—such as, Bikini Kill, Lenny Kravitz, and Relapse Records—are increasingly turning to CASH.

Recently, for instance, CASH played a role in the explosion that is Run the Jewels. I had the opportunity to discuss this with Run the Jewels' manager, Amaechi Uzoigwe:

George Howard: How does CASH fit into your overall strategy?

Amaechi Uzoigwe: While Run the Jewels is able to work successfully with traditional partners like record labels, we're still very much a DIY operation in both spirit and action. Our general approach focuses on strategic relationships that align with our core ethos plus business goals, and ideally delivers value to both us and our audience.

More than anything, we've been able to build a business around good will (i.e. giving the music away for free) and creating a value exchange with our audience that's been very rewarding (hopefully for both sides!) Achieving that hasn't been easy, nor has finding the type of partners who truly understand and embrace our POV but we've been lucky. CASH is a perfect example of that.

GH: Give me some specifics on how you utilize the tools that CASH provides?

AU: The relationship Run the Jewels has with its fans is sacrosanct and managing that relationship is of primary importance, which means we need to exercise as much control over all facets of it as possible. CASH helps us achieve this.

From powering our free download, to site development & design, to mailing list management to analytics, they provide the kind of platform that helps an operation like ours to gain the type of autonomy and empowerment we're looking for, and within a context that feels right for us.

GH: What are the challenges, and how does CASH address them?

AU: While the digital ecosystem has evolved greatly over the past few years, there's still a long way to go until it truly coheres, so for those of us who've charted a course of independence, the journey can be a bit more challenging, but also potentially much more rewarding. Choosing the right kind of partners and platforms is critical to that end. I feel really fortunate to be working with an organization like CASH to help our digital growth, and not simply because they're incredibly smart and cool people who care deeply about music & artists, but because they do great work and deliver the tools that make their passion a reality for many of us.

BENJI ROGERS' .BC CODEC: A FAIR TRADE APPROACH TO MUSIC AND VIRTUAL REALITY USING THE BLOCKCHAIN

Dec 17, 2015

> "I want 2016 to be the year that we do not discuss payouts ever again."

So says Benji Rogers, Founder and CEO of PledgeMusic. I couldn't agree more. In part one of our free-wheeling conversation, we discuss how a combination of Blockchain technology and Virtual Reality could lead to obviating these types of discussions. Part two of the conversation focuses on the more granular specifics of Mr. Rogers' approach.

Big ideas from smart people require more time and words than the "tl;dr" treatment which is *de rigueur,* and I'm pleased to present them to those who care in the format they deserve.

Given the fact that the thousands of words that Ms. Heap and I foisted upon the world have generated not only thousands of views, but also the foundation for the entire *Blockchain for the Arts* movement to build upon, I'm encouraged to keep plunging the depths.

Mr. Rogers and his ideas are certainly worthy of this depth-plunging treatment. Benji Rogers very much epitomizes the notion of finding solutions to problems rather than just moaning about problems and pointing fingers at real or imagined villains. The solutions that Mr. Rogers finds tend to involve using technology to help artists create sustainable careers on their own terms.

As Mr. Rogers noted during our recent conversation, both he and I share **"an unhealthy vision or idea that *better is possible,* and we have yet to achieve it. And, it's driving us both fucking crazy."**

Mr. Rogers is right that he and I *do* share this vision that better is possible, and it *does* tend to lead us both to something resembling megalomania in terms of the amount of time and attention we devote. However, he sells himself short by saying he hasn't yet achieved it.

While there are many miles to go, Mr. Rogers *has* achieved a lot. He is the founder and CEO of PledgeMusic, which is the premiere direct-to-fan music platform, and as such has made tremendous progress towards this goal of enabling artists to have sustainable careers on their own terms.

Technologies such as Blockchain, as well as a recalibration of music as an integral part of a more expansive offering — such as through deeper connections to services like music therapy (which I've written a lot about in this space)—provide reasons for optimism with respect to music's potential for financial health for a wide number of participants.

Mr. Rogers' own form of optimism manifests itself via a combination of the above. Recently, he published a fantastic piece that makes the point that as VR emerges, music will axiomatically play a key role.

As such, the VR industry will desire the most efficient mechanism to integrate music into their offerings. The current approach for music in VR would involve an expensive and time-consuming licensing process that, generally, cannot be done at scale, and thus will only be affordable to larger players.

A system that obviates these high transaction costs, while not violating the existing copyright laws, would create a more expansive market both for the VR companies *and* musicians. Mr. Rogers' solution for how to get there involves utilizing Blockchain technology, and an entirely new codec for music.

In summary, rather than having songs encoded in .mp3 or .AIFF formats, those musicians and labels who desire to have their music more easily ingested into VR applications would use Mr. Rogers' ".bc" codec. This .bc codec would allow artists to utilize smart contracts to ascribe a set of rules and rates for how and at what cost their songs could be used.

The genius of Mr. Rogers' idea, in my opinion, is that, rather than fighting the massive amounts of institutional and technical debt surrounding licensing of music from incumbents, the .bc codec would provide a simple opt-in solution: use the .bc codec and set your own rates and rules, and thus facilitate your music's usage or don't. If you don't...fine...you can continue to license using the existing methods—best of luck.

In this manner, of course, it will be those who have the most to gain and least to lose—independent artists—who jump on the train first. This avoids the often-fatal process of trying to get incumbents to adopt a new technology. If these first movers find success and a two-sided market between those offering their works using the .bc codec and those ingesting their works for VR applications emerges, the incumbents will still have the opportunity to come along for the ride.

The final crucial point about Mr. Rogers' idea is that the VR application of the .bc codec is really a Trojan horse for a broader application. As more content holders embrace this codec in order to have their music used in VR applications, the codec will gain traction in other applications as well. At that point, music users/consumers *of all stripes* will have a choice to make: do we use music that we know—because of the .bc codec—is authenticated by the artist/rights holder, and that stipulates how and at what rate it could be used, or do we ignore this and recode it in whatever way we choose.

In this way, a spectrum emerges with .bc representing a "Fair Trade" music source on one side and other codecs representing "sweatshop" music sources.

Mr. Rogers articulates all of this in our conversation below, which has been edited only lightly for clarity and grammar. In Part 2, Mr. Rogers gets specific about the .bc codec and how we solve the problem of the 40 million songs already in existence.

George Howard: Alright. Great. So, I am psyched to be talking to my friend and sort of partner-in-crime in terms of trying to help artists build sustainable careers on their own terms, Mr. Benji Rogers. Benji, introduce yourself for me, please.

Benji Rogers: Hi. I am Benji, CEO of a company called Pledge-

Music. Frequent flyer and coffee drinker.

GH: I think we are both highly caffeinated at this point. Alright. So, I don't want to talk about Pledge Music. I love PledgeMusic. I use Pledge Music. Thank you for starting Pledge Music. Artists everywhere are in your debt. However, you and I both share an…

BR: …Unhealthy.

GH: You and I both share an unhealthy… what? What is the unhealthy thing that we share?

BR: I think it's an unhealthy vision or idea that better is possible, and we have yet to achieve it. And, it's driving us both fucking crazy.

GH: You got it. That is it exactly. And over the past two years for me, and I don't know how long for you, the unhealthy obsession that might lead to this "better" involves a technology called Blockchain.

And there are an enormous number of articles out there explaining it. So, I don't want to go through the whole thing about the distributed ledger and all that.

I want to talk about a specific sort of impetus that you are working hard on, that you have written about, and that you and I have talked about. So, describe the vision that you have got for this .bc codec.

BR: The idea for a .bc codec arrived in my head when I was trying to solve the problem of creating a data set that was attached to, and that could not be removed from, its content. So, if I made music and I want to ascribe attributes to it, if I want to say that I owned it, say that I could be paid here, say that this was who the publisher was and the songwriter was—there was no way to do that in which it [all of that information] couldn't just be stripped out and the music still be played.

GH: Let me break that down for everybody. So, right now, you take a song and put it into a format, say MP3. You are not able to ascribe or delineate any specific right—who wrote the song, who is the owner of the samples in the song, any of those things. It's just a blob of 1's and 0's around the song itself.

BR: Exactly. One of the cruelest things that you could do to someone back in the day was that you could basically hit Command-I all on their iTunes library and you could change all the metadata on their music.

Now, that's been happening for years and years. And so, what that means is the MP3 or ACC or WAV or MP4 or these formats that are used are inherently changeable, and that's the reason that most of these pirate sites exist—because they are not subject to anything that data says.

GH: Because you can change it.

BR: Because you can change it. Yeah.

GH: I remember this. So, I go and hit Command-I on a song, and there is all of your metadata tagging whatever the hell you want.

BR: You could add a new picture, lyrics...whatever you want.

GH: I wrote "Imagine," not John Lennon. And that gets tethered to the songs, and then I upload it and somebody downloads that song and says, "Wow, I didn't know George Howard wrote 'Imagine.' I thought John Lennon did first."

BR: And, for a while you were getting porn pushed into song files at certain times. What it was, was that it was inherently unstable.

And, then I was kind of pontificating: what if you could create a format that was basically under the moniker of "Fair Trade," and it was where an artist could say: "I am expressing my music into this format. And, attached to that format is a set of rights...the minimum viable data set. Once those rights are in there, I would like for any player that comes across this codec, or this format, to be unable to play it unless it references those rights."

So, if you strip the music away and try and play it somewhere else, you would have to move it to an MP3 or ACC or a WAV. That would mean that the .bc or dot Blockchain codec would become the "Fair Trade" version, making the dot MP3 a kind of sweatshop version, as in it hasn't got my rights expressed into it, therefore I choose not to use it.

Now, as an artist, you could also say, "Copy to an MP3 if you want, that's your choice."

GH: I've got to unpack it, because it is great and it is dense. So, you are saying…the term of art for this would be a "smart contract," you as an artist, just like in the old Command-I manner for Apple iTunes, you would say, "OK, these are the rights around this song. This is what one can do with it. This is what one can't do."

And then you create what you referred to as a "codec." What people need to understand is that could be AIFF or MP3, but this one is on the Blockchain. It would only play on devices that could read this codec, and, because of that, you are sort of doing this handshake that says: **"I, the person who is playing this music, value the music in a Fair Trade way. In the same way as I drink Fair Trade coffee, I value the producer of it." It doesn't mean that you can't strip it out and play it as an MP3, but if you are doing that, you are just sort of affirmatively saying, "I don't value Fair Trade music, I value sweatshop music." Is that right?**

BR: Yes. You are going against the specific wish of the artist, who has chosen to use a format that is fair and equitable to all. It will still sound great. It will still play on your player. It will still do all of those things, because what happens is when an artist creates something they often want it to go as wide as possible, and that's absolutely fine. But there is no way to track it or where it has gone.

Whereas in this case, if the player syncs to the Blockchain, and checks out what is possible for this album or this entire body of work, you can do it. It's not just about the one song. It is about all of your output.

Then what you can do is ascribe a monetary value that is fair and equitable to you as the artist.

What I think this solves is platforms like YouTube and SoundCloud and Spotify… they don't ever get questioned about anything anymore. Because if they are supporting these formats, then they can basically pay exactly who needs to be paid, when they need to be paid. It is not a question of finding any of that information.

You know, I want 2016 to be the year that we do not discuss payouts ever again.

GH: And so, if they are to be believed, [Spotify, et al.] are saying: "We want to pay people. We just can't figure out how." Right? And, my line on that, to some of them, is: "Yeah, you are Google. You *can* figure this out."

This would obviate that. This would then be the grail that I and Andy Weissman and a lot of people have been tilting at for a long time: assume no change in copyright; create smart contracts that are machine readable; allow people to set prices for it. Then, a blossoming of the music business emerges. This isn't a new idea.

What you've done—your iteration on this is—"Yes, great George. Great Andy Weissman...but you need a unified codec and structure...a unified protocol."

And that protocol that you have come up with is this .bc protocol.

BR: It's the .bc protocol, and one of the big problems that the creation of or change to any new database (whether it is distributed or not) has surfaced is "the day zero" problem. Right? Which is: how do you go back to forty million songs?

GH: You don't.

BR: Ultimately.

GH: The answer to that is that you don't. And by that, it doesn't mean that you don't care. Every unified database that anybody has ever tried to pull off but failed has shown that you don't.

So, it has got to be a leading edge moving forward and then sucking those things back into it. How are you going to do that?

In Part 2, Mr. Rogers gets specific about the .bc codec and how we solve the problem of the 40 million songs already in existence.

BENJI ROGERS GETS SPECIFIC ABOUT THE .BC CODEC: A FAIR TRADE MUSIC AND VR SOLUTION USING BLOCKCHAIN

Dec 30, 2015

Giving artists choices and unlocking value from heretofore ignored sources is something PledgeMusic CEO and Founder, Benji Rogers does very well. Mr. Rogers has now turned his focus to the creation of a new music format—the .bc codec—that utilizes Blockchain technology and Virtual Reality to facilitate music licensing, usage for willing participants, and to drag slow moving incumbents to the party.

In Part 1 of our conversation on this topic, Mr. Rogers and I examined the general value proposition of the .bc codec. In Part 2, we dive into the specifics of how the .bc codec could obviate the high transaction costs around the licensing and usage of music while not violating the existing copyright laws, and, as a result, create a more expansive market both for the VR companies and musicians.

Of course, VR is just the beginning. As more content holders embrace this codec in order to have their music used in VR applications, the codec will gain traction in other applications. At that point, music users/consumers of all stripes will have a choice to make:

"Do they use music that they know—because of the .bc codec—is authenticated by the artist/rights holder, and that stipulates how and at what rate it could be used, or do they ignore this and recode it in whatever way they choose?"

In this manner, a spectrum emerges with .bc representing a "Fair Trade" music source on one side, and other codecs representing "sweatshop" music sources.

We pick up our conversation—which has been edited only lightly for clarity and grammar—discussing how the .bc codec could solve the "day zero" problem: the large amounts institutional cruft in the form of bad data that it makes the task of introducing a new approach a very daunting one.

BR: And, so, the way that I proposed [dealing with the "Day One" problem] is through the adoption of VR and AR, which we are looking at basically, coming into being...

GH: Virtual reality and augmented reality. Yeah. So, go ahead.

BR: Being about thirty billion [dollar market] for VR, let's call that hopefully; and then one hundred and fifty for AR, apparently. That's billion. But either way, companies like Oculus, Google, Samsung and Microsoft are all working towards this new technology and are betting heavy and hard on it working.

The idea that came to me was: if I want to make a new piece of art for say Oculus, and I want the audio to match the visual side; to go back and license everything in the old fashioned way is just going to take forever. To solve this problem, I want this file served to me using a codec so that I can basically set it and forget it.

So, I believe that when you are making your next movie in VR and you want to use The Doors' "Strange Days," you will basically go and see if it's [ascribed in the .bc codec].

If it's not, you will put it into this new [.bc] format.

The concept is that every time a new piece or an old piece of music is encoded it auto creates a global distributed database of rights at source.

GH: So, let's play this through. So, I am creating a VR whatever—game or movie. I need music. In today's world, I need to go to the rights holders.

I need to go to the copyright owner of the sound recording, which is typically a label. And, I need to go to the copyright holder of the composition, which is typically a publisher. Long, painful, arduous process. Right?

BR: Paper contracts going back and forth.

GH: Yes. Paper contracts, faxes, phone calls...all sorts of archaic technology. You are saying: we can obviate that by…what?

BR: So, essentially, the way I would picture it is: labels will be incentivized to start to encode in this new codec because they will know that once they have done that there is a central, easy point of contact for their catalog.

If they do not choose to do that, which is highly likely, then what would happen is as you are going to license the music, the VR content owners would say, "We only accept ingestion in this [.bc] format, therefore we need this amount of data in order to be able to play the file."

GH: So, it's very much the idea of: "Hey music guys, VR is *the* thing. If you want your music used in these things and to make lots of money and to get lots of promotion, this is the codec which we will accept. Because we know if we do that, we can do this efficiently. We can track it. We can make the payment. If you do not, okay, we will find something else. Because we bet…"—and this has been my theory forever—"…we bet that there are artists out there who increasingly have their own rights that might want to play in this party." Right?

BR: Absolutely. If you were to spin that another way, picture it this way: "If we don't do this, and VR and AR start to grab UGC content or they grab MP3s or ACCs, combine them with video files and then what you've got is mass takedown notices at scale."

GH: They have already seen the nightmares of that, right? And, this is exactly my point about how Soundcloud has in some respect really harmed music as an investable opportunity. Soundcloud does everything right from the user experience—gets lots of users, people like it—but then, because of the vagaries of music licensing, it seems as if they've got no exit.

BR: And when we look at Soundcloud, it is to say to them, "OK.

Allow me to upload and adopt this format. Therefore, you will know exactly what to do when the time is right."

GH: Yes. And that has been my thesis. Why would Soundcloud, not, at the very minimum, do a skunkworks project and say, "We are going to do one percent of our catalog on the Blockchain and see how it goes."

And the answer to that is because they are busy with other stuff. They don't have the economic motivation to do that.

What you are saying is with VR as an emerging opportunity, they don't have all that technical debt. They don't have all sort of institutional cruft.

It's like "No, we need to start afresh. Let's do it with this codec."

And because of the amount of money around VR, people are going to have to go: "You know what? Now I have to put aside my allegiances or whatever to whatever format and play with this one." And this becomes a sort of tip-of-the-spear, and it eventually drags others into it.

BR: Yeah. That's it. That's exactly it. Yeah.

GH: I hope it happens. So, the things that takes us out of the realm of pie-in-the-sky is just how fast VR is moving, how everybody does believe it's going to be a thing, and how music and other digital rights (but, music is always sort of a Trojan horse or the canary in a coal mine or whatever) is massively important to it.

Right?

BR: I mean, the most important thing is that if you have ever gone into VR, or if you have looked at it, it doesn't make much sense without the sound. Part of me was thinking, "How many licensing deals mentioned 360 degree sound that will change when you move your head?" So either way, there is going to be a way to license that the content owners are going to make it difficult because that's how they make money quite often.

GH: But, my hope is what you are solving. There is an inflection point where [incumbent labels and publishers] will be difficult and operate on layers of scarcity because they believe that that is a better financial mechanism. And, hopefully what you are solving has enough pop to where they go, "Oh, we can make more money doing it this way."

You are an altruistic guy. I am an altruistic guy. But, it is naive to think that they are going to do this for virtuous reasons.

BR: I agree. The one thought that I had—and you and I seem to talk about porn every time we talk—the porn industry is an example embracing this type of codec by saying that we are only going to put it into this type of format if you want the full experience, and if you want it in VR.

The other thing to think about is how many people are going to want to hack and jailbreak the VR players in the next five to ten years. If we make it easy now, you obliterate the need for that. Basically, you can set the content price low or high enough —or whatever you want to do—but it's at the choice of the content owners.

I think that if I were to own a catalog, I'd want it to be in the most accessible format possible to the next generation of players

GH: Yeah. Right. Of course. This is my "taco shop" analogy. I own a taco shop and I've got $5,000 a year to pay for music, and all that I really want is Texas Tornados and stuff like that. I don't want fucking Coldplay.

But you can't set the market-clearing price and get it that way.

To pull back just for one second, I think today on Engadget the headline was*:* "Rockband VR is coming from Oculus and Harmonics in 2016." It will be the leading edge.

And somebody is furiously trying to figure out what massive licensing deal needs to take place to ingest music into it.

Is it a sync? Is it a public performance? What is it? How do we do it? And, the answer is: nobody really knows.

And so we are going to cram it into the DMCA and other things, which is going to cause lots of confusion and everything else.Why not let content holders just say, "Here is the price for which I will allow these types of usages to take place?"

There will be a moment of arbitrage. There will be a moment where people will be underpricing and overpricing, and people will take advantage of that. But, the markets will eventually set marketing clearing prices.

BR: And, also you and I talked about this. We have seen this sort of that early stage Monegraph talking about it in visual works. One of the things that you and I have discussed is that the technology is all here. It just hasn't been combined in this format. One of the hopes of writing a piece and talking to you and kind of getting out there was like:

Let's make a Fair Trade standard. Let's stick to that and say as content creators and people that build things and make things, "This is fair to us. Interact with it as you see fit, according to these rules. If you want other rules, break them. But, then you are going against my wishes as a creator. And that's my choice to create something in this way."

[Disclosure: George Howard is an advisor to and shareholder of Monegraph]

GH: And that obviates the sort of stick in the mud people out there who are like: "Well, Blockchain is just another thing."

It's like, yeah…kind of. But, it's an immutable database that doesn't obviate rule of law. It does allow for people to make a choice.

And that is sort of where we are moving.

The burden on some of that is on you and me, or whatever, to help customers understand what's going on there. To quote Michael Roberston: "Look at what the NFL has done. It used to be that you could only watch football games on Sundays and Mondays, right? Now, people watch them all the time, and engage through Fantasy Leagues. And, it's only grown."

His point is: if we were to give people more music, they will want more music. Right?

What [the .bc codec] addresses is that it allows people to make choices about how they are going to access it. It uses the money and the technology to actually define and drive this codec because it will make everybody's life easier.

BR: Yeah. And, I think also from the artist's perspective... I've been in the artist's shoes for most of my life, and when you are about to print something from your studio, whether it is coming out of portals or going into digital for the first time, what you are doing is you're saying, "OK, I want this to go to...,"You have the uses in your head for your album, right? Or for your piece of art. And then what you realize is: it will be taken and mashed up in any which way.

Now, what I love is this thought that a company like Dubset, where they are going to scan for EDM mixes. So, EDM mixes can be created. But as long as those markers and identifiers are still within them, you track it wherever they go. There's a beautiful moment where you can sit there and say, "I want to negotiate with this artist directly for their song. Do it."

GH: And, you can do that through smart contracts. I think people will get bogged down in questioning how that can scale. No. No. No. The artist will over time delineate the use cases at the prices and the users will connect with them at scale.

BR: Yeah. Yeah. Absolutely. And, I think it is also just the simple thought of like saying, "If I put it up on Soundcloud, they don't respect the rights today. But if I put it up on this platform, it does."

Then, people will know to go and make that choice. It's the same thing as when I met my favorite coffee shop owner. I said, "Why is your coffee two bucks more expensive?" And he said, "Because I don't want five year olds picking the berries that I serve. I just don't want that."

And I think that when someone says, "Why are you paying twenty-four dollars for this new streaming service that doesn't even exist yet? You say, "It's because the artists have said this is what they are backing."

GH: I was talking to my friend who was somewhere in fucking—I don't know if these places actually exist—Montana. Is that a place? And...

BR: I have been there. It's strange.

GH: He was saying, "My friends who own bars, they won't deal with ASCAP or BMI. They now go to local bands and say: 'we want to play the music in our bars. Let's make some kind of deal;' whether that deal is we are just going to have your CD's here or we will sell your t-shirts or whatever."

That's where we are moving. And so, this just allows that to move at scale.

BR: Yeah. I am one hundred percent with you there. I think it's...and you know, you have that Buy Local day...It's like Buy Fair Trade, or experience Fair Trade for the first time, is what it will be.

Because it will be an audiovisual experience in which you as the user are sitting there saying, "Wow." Everyone in the chain is taken care of here: the visual rights owner, the songwriter, the publisher... all the way through, and if you want to go outside of that bound that is your right.

And when I say, "Making MP3 a sweat shop format," I mean it is just going to be a choice that you make. If you want to buy a crappy t-shirt that was made in a sweat shop because you don't care...go for it.

But if you are an artist, you should at least have one route that you can express, "This is my choice."

It would be great for live albums. After you are finished playing, this is going to be available to everybody through this portal. "Go get it. Have fun. Awesome!"

GH: And just to be really clear, that portal could be a billion portals. Anybody that wants to sell a live album could utilize this codec to sell it through their devices as well.

BR: Absolutely.

GH: Benji, you are great.

BR: You are great, too.

GH: We need more minds like yours in the music business. Thank you so much for doing this.

BR: Thank you for having me.

MEDIACHAIN FACILITATES AUTOMATIC ATTRIBUTION USING BLOCKCHAIN AND MACHINE LEARNING

Jul 29, 2016

With all the promise around Blockchain Tech (and there *is* a ton of promise), there is also—as there is with any nascent technology—a host of open questions. These bugaboos provide fodder for doubters, but also force good faith proponents to really hone their products, POVs, and arguments.

As all readers of this space know, I'm certainly a proponent, but as some readers of this space do not appear to see, I attempt to not only "cheerlead" this technology, but also to push and prod around the issues—obvious or otherwise—that might, at worst, be its undoing, but, in all cases, must be addressed.

For some time, for instance, I've been concerned about what I call the "Garbage In/Garbage Out" problem related to Blockchain tech. That is, in no circumstance does Blockchain tech obviate the problems around people registering information on the Blockchain that they do not have the rights to (by the way, this same exact issue plagues pretty much every system; for instance, I could submit a copyright registration for the song "Single Ladies," and I'd likely receive a registration number).

In fact, arguably, Blockchain tech—due to its efficiencies—might actually amplify problems around infringing or fraudulent works being registered on this type of ledger. Certainly, numerous efforts are under-way to address this "Garbage In" problem through any number of innovative methods; from authentication of origin via a series of steps that are delightful for fans to engage in, but difficult/impossible for bots to replicate, to purer technologically-based solutions.

However, until recently, I'd not seen anyone addressing the other end of the spectrum. That is, when content is downloaded and then altered, any type of tracking can be broken relatively easily. This content can then be re-registered with different/false credentials in order to essentially "break the chain."

I was delighted, therefore, to learn from my good friend, Andy Weissman (who contributed one of the best interviews I've had the good fortune to post on this topic, and is still very much recommended if you're looking for a succinct primer on how Blockchain Tech can address issues around copyright), of a firm called Mediachain.

Once intrigued, I set out to learn more via interviewing Mediachain's founders, Denis Nazarov and Jesse Walden. I was further delighted when I learned that one of the founders, Jesse Walden, has a background as a successful artist manager, and therefore not only understands the complexities around these issues from a real-world perspective, but is motivated to solve them from an "artist-first" point of view.

[The entire interview, lightly edited for content, is below.]

George Howard: Give me a little background—what led you to this place? I know you guys don't have the typical (whatever that means) backgrounds that tend to lead to starting/running a Blockchain Tech company.

Denis Nazarov: Before becoming a software engineer, I received a BFA and worked as a professional photographer. In the classical tradition, I was taught to create one-of-a-kind masterpieces that were meant to hang on the walls of galleries. Around the same time, platforms like Facebook, Tumblr, and Instagram had begun to become the dominant ways of consuming visual information. Media on these platforms spread so quickly and widely, often without credit for the author. The notion of creativity and authorship was completely turned on its head. People quickly became obsessed with the feed, instead of caring about creators or their works.

Instead of contributing to the noise, I became fascinated with how content propagates the internet, and decided I wanted to build better publishing tools and platforms that would actually empower creators and their audiences.

Jesse Walden: Before embarking on this project, I co-founded an artist management company where I represented independent musicians including Solange Knowles, Blood Orange, Majical Cloudz, and others. I was entrenched in a host of problems to-do with music data, which can be summarized by saying that all the information about who made or owns music is fractured across zillions of proprietary databases, preventing artists from being paid and making life difficult for services wanting to pay them.

Early in the life of the project, we were inspired by two things: the implications of Bitcoin for a new generation of completely open and decentralized data storage, and the magic of the technologies behind Shazam and Google Image Search to let us know the artist of an image or the song at a click of a button.

DN: Everyone at Mediachain Labs came up during the file sharing free-for-all of the early aughts. From Napster to BitTorrent, Megaupload to Tumblr, over just the course of a decade, we were front row as new communities developed around the massive corpus of art being reproduced online.

All the content was there if you knew where to look, but the connection to the creator wasn't.

Digital media was incredibly easy to distribute, but incredibly difficult to trace. New platforms eventually caught up to offer legitimate services, but the result was a loss of innovation at the hands of newly powerful distributors that created new silos, often to the detriment of creators and their audiences.

What brought us together was the shared passion for supporting creativity, sharing, and belief in the contextual nature of cultural experience.

GH: Fantastic, I love the origin story. I, as writer/academic/investor/consultant have been pushing on the distributed ledger topic for quite some time now, and, on one hand, feel like the space is maturing a bit, and on the other still feel like it's very formative. While I have my own efforts in the space that I'm hoping will provide use cases that really represent case studies/best practices, I'm curious—generally, what you feel the current state of the art with respect to Blockchain tech is?

JW: Blockchain has become a buzzword, commanding enormous attention, thought, and investment. The innovation of Blockchain is enabling distributed consensus without needing to trust a central authority. Until recently, this has been possible at the cost of performance, making Blockchains powering Bitcoin and Ethereum ineffectual for the scale of data associated with media and culture. Writes take a long time, capacity is small, and each update has a financial cost. Every participant must replicate all contents of the chain, even if there is useless data.

While this is important to prevent "double spending" of digital currencies, it is unnecessary for the use case of collaboratively tracking and identifying media and its descriptive metadata. For this use case, it's useful to define "Blockchain" as a metaphor for decentralized and open data, while aiming for an implementation that is also capable of scaling at low cost and preserving the complex relationships and interactions we have with our universal culture.

The state-of-the-art technology that meets those requirements is called IPFS, a peer-to-peer, scalable data network. Mediachain utilizes a Blockchain structure built on top of IPFS, and many other Bitcoin and Ethereum based projects like OpenBazaar are turning to IPFS for a scalable, decentralized data solution. If Blockchain is a metaphor for shared and open data, IPFS is the state of the art implementation with a vibrant open source community to boot.

GH: Excellent. Dense, but in a good and necessary way. Thanks. Building off the above, the "underlying magic" [to steal a Guy Kawasaki phrase] that Mediachain seems to represent addresses one of my bigger bugaboos with respect to Blockchain tech: losing track of the asset.

Specifically, it's all well and good to initiate a registry on the BC, but the moment someone downloads and re-uploads that asset there is a high degree of likelihood that you lose the ability to track the asset. To me this is a critical failure that—like the "garbage in" problem that is my other big issue—if left unresolved greatly limits the applicability of a BC (Bitcoin or otherwise). You've addressed this, right?

JW: Yes. Historically, DRM schemes have attempted to track media by erecting walls, coupling specialized codecs or metadata with proprietary distribution. This artificial scarcity doesn't work due to the free and infinite reproducibility of bits that makes it so easy to spread media across a multitude of distribution channels. Any metadata that is stored with the file—like EXIF, ID3, and other encodings or wrappers—can be easily stripped out and lost. This happens as soon as you take an image from its source and upload it to, for instance, Facebook.

This is why Mediachain uses perceptual recognition technology - similar to Shazam or Google Image search—to identify media based on how it looks or sounds, automatically resolving any instance to information about it in Mediachain. Near duplicate detection is a specialization of machine learning that works very well, even for images that are cropped, distorted, etc.

Rather than erecting walls and aiming to create artificial scarcity, we view decentralization as a means to break walls down and enable more open re-use that aligns with the way information propagates on the internet. Leveraging content identification technology, we can make information about the work, such as who made it, where it was published, and what people are saying about it discoverable anywhere media is found. This is a prerequisite to enabling value to flow. It starts with attention (attribution), gratitude, and analytics, and can lead to financial exchange directly through media itself.

GH: Yes, yes! This sums up so much. I've been saying forever that this type of tech will and should enable—as you say—or unlock value flow.

So…tell me about your road map/progress. Congratulations on the funding - particularly, as some of it's coming from my favorite VC in the world, my friend Andy Weissman—but now the real work begins, right…what's next? Are you at MVP/POC?

JW: Today, over two million images or related metadata records have been contributed to Mediachain by organizations that embrace open access, including MoMA, Getty Images, the Digital Public Library of America, and others.

Getty Images, for example, sees Mediachain as a linear extension of their Embed program, which enables free and attributed use of their images for non-commercial purposes. We are excited to help more organizations adopt open access and benefit from the scale of their work's re-use online.

The Mediachain protocol is open source under the MIT License, and we are approaching the launch of an alpha network later this month.

As more media data is contributed to the network, we're excited to see developers start building interesting applications—whether it's an image annotation platform, an application that allows you to listen to music just by having its artwork, or one that lets you buy a product in a photo directly from the maker—and as those applications are built, we'll start to see more interesting data written into the network. This is a really exciting network effect, and because the network is decentralized, it benefits all participants rather than a central entity.

GH: Right, and so it seems to me that the notion of a *distributed* ledger—with the "distributed" part being at its core—is so crucial...

JW: Exactly, it's important to note how important decentralization is as a catalyst for Mediachain. Attempts to build a global media database with a centralized consortium or federated design have perverse incentives that require participants to cede control of their data to some third party. The Global Repertoire Database is an infamous example of the political failures that these approaches run into within the highly distributed media ecosystem.

Because Mediachain is completely open and decentralized, it provides a permissionless environment for collaboration and innovation that just wasn't possible before these technologies came to light. The open and decentralized design of Mediachain means anyone can participate, and each participant retains control over their data. We're excited about the opportunities for innovation this infrastructure enables.

GH: Excellent. Thanks so much for taking the time.

PRS FOR MUSIC CEO, ROBERT ASHCROFT, DISCUSSES CHALLENGES AND INNOVATIONS IN MUSIC COLLECTION

Jan 28, 2016

I had the good fortune to moderate a panel during Berklee College of Music's Rethink Music event that included the Chief Executive of PRS for Music, Robert Ashcroft. The panel grew contentious very quickly with respect to the role (or lack thereof) of new technology as it applies to music databases.

Stepping back from the panel for a moment, certainly "the data issue" really is at the heart of the problems of the current music business. Depending on whom you believe:

- *Certain parties have the data and benefit by not sharing it.*
- *No one has accurate data.*
- *Companies could "fix" the data problem, but doing so is not in their interest.*
- *The vast amount of historical data—much of it poorly cataloged (if at all)—makes it a fool's errand to ever attempt to fix the problem.*

Of course, those in other data-heavy industries face similar issues. As we increasingly quantify data at granular levels—for instance, the field of wearables and genomics is really just addressing granular data problems— we are, as Bill Tai so eloquently summed up in my conversation with him, attempting to take heretofore unstructured data and structure it.

Perhaps no part of the music business has a bigger data problem than publishing. While a recording might have a number of performers, there is typically only one label that owns the right to the recording of the song. On the other hand, the rights around the song itself—in music business parlance, "the composition"—are often vastly more complex.

For instance, there might be several writers of a song, and each of these writers might have different publishers (who also have rights to the song), and if the song has a sample in it, this greatly expands the complexities. Of course, a single song also can be recorded by lots of different artists (i.e. be "covered"), which—again—compounds the complexities with respect to who is owed money when the song is played on radio, sold, used in a movie, streamed, etc.

In the UK, PRS for Music represents songwriters, composers, and publishers with respect to the right of public performance of their songs. That is, any time a song is, for instance, played on radio, streamed, broadcast on TV, played in a venue, etc., PRS for Music is responsible for making sure that the songwriters and publishers of that song are paid.

Given this challenge, it was incredibly heartening to have Mr. Ashcroft espouse a technology-forward viewpoint during the panel. So much so, that I was compelled to reach out to him afterwards and request an interview in order to discuss the challenges and opportunities facing not just PRS for Music, but the music business generally, with an eye towards innovative ways to address the data problem.

Mr. Ashcroft was generous with his time and information. We spoke for a good deal of time, and I've broken the transcription of our conversation into several parts, each focusing on specific areas.

Below is part one, in which Mr. Ashcroft and I discuss the challenges detailed above, and Mr. Ashcroft iterates some initiatives that PRS for Music is embarking upon that I genuinely did not ever believe I'd see an institution of the size of PRS for Music take on.

It's a testament to both Mr. Ashcroft's background as a technologist and the forward-looking view of the board of PRS for Music who brought him on that PRS for Music appears to be leading the trail for other institutions of its ilk to follow.

[The interview below has been edited lightly for clarity and grammar.]

George Howard: I am really excited about this particular talk. I am going to ask my guest to introduce himself. So, Robert, tell us a little bit about yourself.

Robert Ashcroft: I am Robert Ashcroft. I am the Chief Executive of PRS for Music, which is the UK's copyright collection society. So, roughly speaking, it is the ASCAP or BMI in the United States.

GH: Great. And, thanks so much for taking the time. I can only imagine how busy you are. We met at a panel that I moderated for the Berklee Rethink event, but before I dive into that, can you give me thirty seconds or so on your background? How did you come to be the CEO of PRS for Music?

RA: Well, I worked at Sony Electronics for eight years. And while I was there, I was in charge of their internet-related businesses, both in the United States where I founded Sonystyle.com, and then in Europe. Not so much the e-commerce, but linking devices to internet services through mobile, text, and broadcast networks. With that technology experience, I was then approached by PRS for Music because the internet and all things related become very important for the music industry. I think they needed a chief executive who knew how to navigate that world.

GH: That explains so much. I am really glad that I asked that question because, as I said, we met on the panel, and contentious is not strong enough a word for it. Contrary to what some of the other panelists may have believed, I really had no objective other than to facilitate a conversation, and it was a conversation about technology in the music business. And, there were a couple of people, or at least one person up there, who were sort of deeply interested in Cryptocurrency generally, and Blockchain specifically. I think people think that I am some sort of evangelist for Blockchain tech. I am really not. I just think it's interesting technology that could provide an answer.

And, I was so deeply impressed by you, as someone in your position, not dismissing Blockchain or any other type of tech as being a potential for addressing some of the issues.

And now that you have given your background, it makes all the sense in the world. So, as you say, this sort of merger of technology and music is coming. And, I think that first questions that I asked you on the panel was: "What's the biggest problem facing your business?"

So, as we sort of weave into my broader question, let's pause on that for a second: what's causing you stress as the CEO of PRS for Music these days?

RA: Well, I think that the biggest issue facing the industry in the internet era is metadata. We will have received notification of a trillion uses of music this year now that individual streams are reported by the individual reporting services—the Spotify, the YouTubes, etc. of this world.

What these guys are streaming are sound recordings. But, sound recordings obviously have ownership of the publishing rights, composers', and songwriter's rights embedded in them, and there are often multiple versions of them. Well, when I say multiple versions, there are rather multiple parties to each one.

GH: I am sorry to interrupt. But, just to be clear, I love how specific you are getting, but in the music business, there are two dominant copyrights: one for the composition —the person that writes the lyrics and the melody— and then there is the copyright to the sound recording, which is the actual version of that song—typically owned by the label or the performer. And then, you are suggesting that there are now derivative works—call them "remixes" or "samples"—of songs where you are mashing these different copyrights together into one work and sample and sort of...

RA: We haven't even gotten there yet.

Even in a standard sound recording, there are other parties. So, what we have to do is we have to know which sound recording is being used. And then we need to work out who has the author's rights and who has the publishing rights to that. So, we have this matching exercise that needs to go on. We try to match the International Standard Recording Code to the International Standard Works Code in order to work out who to pay. And, that exercise requires...

GH: And again, I am sorry to interrupt you, but just for clarity, the ISRC codes and the ISWC Codes are supposed to line up with the different rights holders for those copyrights you just outlined.

RA: Correct. That's right.

GH: In your job, just to pull back for a second, PRS for Music, the UK performance rights organization runs slightly differently than the U.S. versions—which are ASCAP, BMI, and SECSAC—in the sense that you collect, not only for the so-called "right of public performance," which is any type of broadcast (when a song is played on the radio, or on the websites, or in restaurants, etc.) but also for the right of "reproduction and distribution," which would typically be called a "mechanical license." That is the term of art.

RA: Yes, we do. We do so under a contract with MCPS (the Mechanical Copyright Protection Society), which is actually an independent and outsourced business of both licensing and administration to PRS for Music. So, the rights are administered together.

GH: Perfect. So, could you, in plain English, then describe how, if a songwriter has his work or her work used in the U.K.—by that I mean played on the radio, or maybe sold via iTunes, or whatever—do you intersect with those types of usages?

RA: So, what we need to know is: what is the sound recording that has been used? And then we need to match that to the underlying copyright. In other words, who wrote it and who publishes it? That matching exercise requires the accurate metadata.

GH: And so, the flow then is what? In the United States, it's sort of this idea: "I am a songwriter or publisher, and a new work is created. I then register that work with the performance rights organizations with whom I am affiliated. I go online. I send in a form listing my writer's share and my publisher's share."

Is there a similar sort of process in the U.K.?

RA: Yes. That's happily universal.

GH: Right. And you get this mountain of data coming at you from all these songwriters because they have a vested interest, because if they don't do this and their songs are played on the radio, they get nothing. Correct?

RA: That's right. They need to be registered in order to be paid.

GH: So, as we talked about in the beginning, this used to be a less complex landscape than it is today. Why is that? Why is it such a bigger challenge in 2015 than it was in 1995?

RA: Well, first of all, because there is a much larger number of uses in music. In the year before I joined, I think the PRS for Music processed 15 million usages.

GH: What year was that? I'm sorry.

RA: That was in 2010. In 2009, it was about 15 million. And now we are up to one trillion.

GH: Oh, my Lord.

RA: It's going to grow.

GH: Right.

RA: In the old days, let's say a download was a download for life.

The stream is just a moment in time, with a single pair of ears, and it has generated a huge amount of data. So, that's the thing. The other thing is, when you have got that amount of data, people want to be paid out on a transactional basis.

In the old days, when you couldn't get the data, and, indeed today, we don't go around with a clipboard and note down which songs are played in each cafe and bar in the land. We have to do some sort of analogy, and we split the revenue over the determination by analogy. That's "not" acceptable in the internet era.

GH: OK. I want to pause there for a second, because I couldn't agree more. Right. So, this is something that I get when I talk to songwriters or artists, this comes up all the time. When I am trying to explain to them the right of public performance, and I say to them: "Well, look, you go and play in some club, in theory, you are supposed to be paid for that public performance, or if you cover someone's song, the person whose song you are covering is supposed to be paid."

And, the artist I'm explaining this to always goes: "Well, how?"

I say, "Well, there is no really great mechanism. They sort of look at a lot of different things and factor them in, but they are not going to just send out a million people to sit in clubs to look at it."

My own personal opinion is: why not use some Shazam-esque type of device and stick it up in the corner of a club, and even if it is only sixty percent right, that's going to be better than what we are doing.

But, I am fascinated by the fact that you say that is "unacceptable." Because you just don't hear people in your position saying that. So, what are you doing to make this better?

RA: We are engaged in a whole bunch of experiments both in developing technology—we have a particular project that we are running with Google Play at the moment where we are looking at ways of getting the cost of the devices that would be left in premises around the land down to the point to where it is cost effective.

GH: That's my Shazam idea. Right?

RA: That's your Shazam idea.

There are also other specialist companies that have technologies that can be deployed in nightclubs and other venues.

We've got a trial going on at the moment between three competing providers looking for the best and most cost-effective method of using actual song recognition.

In addition to that, we are putting a facility on our website to enable people to record the songs that they play in gigs around the land. We call it the Setlist Hub. And with the technology at our disposal, we try to find ways of gathering data that are more and more accurate.

GH: Okay. So, I am with you. Right. So, two things come to mind: first off, awesome. Glad that's happening. Second, if you succeed at that, that is only going to add more orders of magnitude to your incoming data. Right?

RA: Yes.

GH: The event is going to be sort of an iterative process. With respect to one of the things you said we are going to have—I forget what you call it, "Song Hub" or whatever—where people go in and say, "I played these songs"; it leads me to my fundamental problem with data generally, which is the "garbage in scenario." Whether good faith, or bad faith, somebody puts bad data into the system. Right? And, that must be a massive problem for you, right?

RA: It is. When you think about this SetList Hub idea, if you have an app, both the people are performing and the audience are able to put the data in, then you have some sort of check on the accuracy, just by virtue of the row of numbers. If you were to …

GH: Play that out for me. So, you are saying that the data smoothes out. The outliers smooth out just because of large numbers. Is that what you mean?

RA: Well, that's the theory behind this. If you've enough people reporting then you are more likely to come to the absolute truth, both in terms of accuracy and in terms of knowledge.

GH: So, I didn't understand the premise. So, the premise isn't that the songwriters are putting in the data, it is the fans themselves that are using it?

RA: It's both.

GH: It's both. OK. So, you are sort of crowd-sourcing the metadata. What is the incentive for some customer, or, as you would say in England, "punter," to do this? They are at a show, why are they going to open some app and put the song name in?

RA: It's really simple. People love music.

GH: Well, that's true. So, yes, but…

RA: They want to say, "Hey, I listen to this great song," or "They played so and so."

GH: That's badass. So, I have this theory: all successful internet applications have to be social, fun, and competitive. And competitive is just sort of a "game mechanics" thing. It doesn't mean that you have to win, but you have to get something.

And so, your premise is that people love music. "Hey, this band is playing this thing, and I'm, for some reason, going to add this in," and then you are going to sift through that. I love that! Why is nobody else doing it? Are other people doing this?

RA: I don't know. This is something that we are just experimenting with at the moment. So, if I am brutally honest, our web infrastructure, if you go into our website, then it is not exactly...

GH: I have. It's a nightmare.

RA: It's a nightmare. We've got a huge project, the "Digital Transformation Project," because we have systematically over the years squeezed all the drops of juice out of the lemon and not really reinvested in the technology. We are working in an era now where that is no longer possible. So, we're engaging in all of these things, music recognition technology to set this up, to upgrade the digital nature of our business.

Part VI

THINK PIECES II

We Have The Push, Now We Need The Pull - A 'Blockchain And The Arts' State Of The Union

Canary In A Coalmine: From Internet of Things to VR to Blockchain: How Music Guides Other Industries

How Blockchain Could Help Kanye Use Facebook To Get Out Of Debt - And Solve Facebook's Video Problem

From Modeling To Measuring: A Blockchain Solution For Music At Political Events

Haters Gonna Hate: Why Those Celebrating The "Death" Of The Bitcoin Blockchain Are Missing The Point

WE HAVE THE PUSH, NOW WE NEED THE PULL: A 'BLOCKCHAIN AND THE ARTS' STATE OF THE UNION

Oct 7, 2015

There's a distinct sense that the train has begun to leave the station with respect to Blockchain technology being utilized by artists.

Over the past couple of weeks, I moderated/participated on three panels—The Rethink Fair Music Workshop, MIT's Hacking Arts, and The Music Business Association's Entertainment & Technology Law Conference. While Blockchain technology was the stated theme on only one of these panels (The Music Business Association's panel), it was the dominant topic on *all* of them.

As I tweeted after The Rethink panel, "If contention and passion are precursors to change (I think they are), we're headed in the right direction."

I believe the energy and contention around Blockchain tech are heating up because:

- **We're seeing actual application of the technology.**
- **Those who don't understand the technology/the implications are finding it harder to ignore, and are becoming defensive.**

Aston Motes predicted this defensiveness from incumbents who are threatened by new technology back when I started beating the drum about Blockchain many moons ago, and his tweet inspired me to write a piece entitled: “Bitcoin Can't Save The Music Industry Because the Music Industry Will ResistbTransparency.”

Certainly not all of the incumbents are taking a purely defensive stance; I was deeply impressed, for example, by the open-minded and reasoned views with respect to Blockchain tech expressed by Robert Ashcroft, CEO of PRS, on the Rethink Fair Music Panel.

However, change rarely begins at the institutional level.

Rather, as *The Innovator's Dilemma* observed, change starts at the margin, and (occasionally) crosses the chasm into a wider segment of users. Once the chasm is crossed, it is typically too late for incumbents to embrace the technology that customers are now demanding in increasing numbers (essentially, this is what happened to RIM/Blackberry—and others—with respect to iPhone).

This is why I'm constantly telling incumbents (clients or otherwise) that they are far better off disrupting themselves (via skunkworks, Shooting Star approaches) than being disrupted.

Artists, almost axiomatically, inhabit the margins. Additionally, given the state of the music industry, artists are increasingly embracing the mindset of “what-do-I-have-to-lose” that predicates change. It's understandable, therefore that they are embracing Blockchain technology.

This attitude with respect to Blockchain technology is most visibly articulated by the great Imogen Heap.

Again, many moons ago, I had the distinct pleasure of talking with Ms. Heap regarding her views on the current state of the music industry and her then-nascent conceptions on how Blockchain technology could have a role in the future.

Ms. Heap has now put action to words and released her work, "Tiny Human," utilizing Blockchain technology. This is an actual, real world example of an artist "pushing" a work out that utilizes elements of Blockchain technology—such as, so called, smart contracts, which are machine readable.

With this gesture, we've now moved beyond the realm of the theoretical.

These machine-readable smart contracts are the most exciting elements of Blockchain technology. For instance, by utilizing this technology, an artist can clearly delineate what she will allow others to do with her works, and at what price, if any.

An example is instructive:

The following is taken from the "Licensing Help" section of the ASCAP website. ASCAP represents songwriters' public performance rights:

^ I'm interested in playing music in my restaurant or other business. I know that I need permission for live performances. Do I need permission if I am using only CD's, records, tapes, radio or TV?

Yes, you will need permission to play records or tapes in your establishment. Permission for radio and television transmissions in your business is not needed if the performance is by means of public communication of TV or radio transmissions by eating, drinking, retail or certain other establishments of a certain size which use a limited number of speakers or TVs, and if the reception is not further transmitted (for example, from one room to another) from the place in which it is received, and there is no admission charge. Your local ASCAP licensing manager can discuss your needs and advise how ASCAP can help you.

Today, if you decide to open a taco shop, and you want to play your collection of Texas Tornados CDs or downloads in your taco shop to set the mood, there are hoops you must jump through, and costs.

There is certainly nothing wrong with those who desire to play music having to get the approval of the artists whose works they desire to play, and to compensate them fairly to do so.

The problem lies in the inefficiencies of the systems.

The taco shop owner may only want to play the music of The Texas Tornados or other music that fits the mood of his shop, **but he is *required to buy a blanket license that gives him the right to play anything in the PRO's catalog*; he is essentially paying for music he doesn't want/will likely never play.**

Similarly, The Texas Tornados might love to have their music played not just in this taco shop, but in any number of other places that would benefit from playing their music. (Really, who wouldn't benefit from playing the music of the Texas Tornados?) The Texas Tornados might even be willing to set a price that would encourage people to utilize their music.

But, they don't get to set the price. ASCAP does.

An alternative method that utilizes Blockchain technology would be:

- The Texas Tornados create a set of rules with respect to how their song and recording could be used and at what price (certainly, in the case of the Texas Tornados, there are complications around this with respect to co-writers/labels/publishers/etc. **but, as Ms. Heap has shown us, there are increasing numbers of artists without these institutional constraints).**

- They ascribe these rules in a smart contract on the Blockchain in a manner that can be read by machines.
- The taco shop owner determines that he wants music that fits the mood of his taco shop, and delineates a set of categories and descriptions. Additionally, the taco shop owner determines what amount he is willing to spend each year on this music.
- The taco shop owner—using an interface—does a search for works that match these criteria (essentially an RFP).
- When a match is found, the song is playable, and the rights holders are paid based on usage.

In this approach, there is no need for a performance rights organization such as ASCAP or BMI. The content creator sets a price and set of usages related to his work; the content user either accepts (and pays) these prices and is able to use the work, or does not.

This is just one—admittedly, overly-simplistic—example to illustrate the possibilities. However, it hints at the vast array of potential uses that are possible with this technology.

It won't start at the institutional level, but it will start.

There will be a skateboard shop (or gaming shop or coffee

shop) that derives benefit—both from a financial perspective and a marketing perspective—from deciding to only use music that is available via machine readable smart contracts, that allow them to pick precisely the music they want from artists (and they won't want mainstream artists...at first) at a price that is both fair for the skate shop and the artist, and delight in the fact that they're connecting directly with the artist.

More succinctly: to paraphrase what my friend Andy Weissman said on one of the above-mentioned panels, **"Right now, we have essentially three music streaming services. We should have thousands."**

His meaning is that Blockchain technology—in a similar manner to the taco shop example (and more cogently articulated by Mr. Weissman himself in my interview with him, entitled "Union Square Ventures' Andy Weissman On the Blockchain And the Music Rights 'Nirvana State'")—will enable anyone who wants to set up a streaming service to do so.

So, this is where we are. Via Ms. Heap and others, we're starting to get a push of content that is utilizing Blockchain technology. What we need next are those taco shops and a billion other use cases to start creating the pull.

CANARY IN A COALMINE: FROM INTERNET OF THINGS TO VR TO BLOCKCHAIN: HOW MUSIC GUIDES OTHER INDUSTRIES

Dec 31, 2015

As a rule, I wish futurists would just go to the future and stop annoying those of us here in the present. Thus, I tend to avoid prognostication. Increasingly, however, my vocations require me to—paraphrasing my wise friend, Venture Capitalist, Andy Weissman—envision and bet on a future I'd like to see come to fruition in the next three to five years.

Still, it seems hollow to use this space to just "predict" what 2016 holds for the music business. Instead, I'd like to mostly invert the normative predictive New Year's Eve trope, and return to a theme I often espouse: **the music business is a canary in the coalmine for other industries. As goes the music industry, so goes other industries.**

Participants in non-music industries, therefore, would be wise to view the music business as a cautionary tale.

I first put forth this Canary in a Coalmine idea back in the summer of 2010 on my personal blog, 9GiantSteps.com:

I truly believe that the music business is a canary in a coalmine, and, therefore, it's wise to view the travails and successes of the music business and see what you might be able to avoid/apply in whatever work you do.

My dominant theme at the time of this initial writing was that innovation often occurs in the music space prior to other industries. In large part, this is because of music's relatively small file sizes and its appeal to college students, who have a combination of more time than money and access to high speed internet.

Streaming:

My thesis at the time has been borne out. I stated that streaming would become a prominent part of people's lives—both for music and video—in a much more rapid fashion than most expected.

Similarly, I predicted that cloud-based applications—the "cloud", of course, being just another version of streaming, but semantically better applied to data/"work" than entertainment—would also become quickly prominent.

These positions were put forth in two different, but similarly titled, posts:

The Stream that Snuck up on You (2010)
The Cloud That Snuck up on You (2012)

Sharing Economy:

While envisioning music as a leading edge for streaming/cloud-based computing is a fairly straightforward analogy, music's most important predictive of the past few years is less readily apparent.

The innovations in the music business that led to both P2P file sharing and DAWs (like ProTools), and resulted in the dawn of the age of disintermediation —removing any mid-

dlemen that stand between content creators and content consumers—is truly only now picking up speed across industries.

The ability for a musician to easily and cheaply create their works and then present them to consumers without myriad institutions—labels, promoters, distributors, retailers—standing between, is similar both in spirit and mechanics not only to the relatively parallel analogies of people creating movies, documentaries, instructional videos, podcasts, books, blogs, etc. and disseminating directly to consumers with few or no middlemen, but also to more orthogonal industries.

For instance, Uber, Airbnb, Taskrabbit, Etsy, and other ventures that are generally lumped under the heading of "sharing economy," all trade in the same disintermediated approach that was first prominently visible in the music industry. Uber, et al. facilitate the unlocking of assets - either surplus personal goods (cars/spare bedrooms for Uber and Airbnb) or time/homemade goods (Taskrabbit, Etsy)—that heretofore required layers of institutional involvement to do so.

And, just as the road to disintermediated music business nirvana has been paved with recalcitrant incumbents clinging mightily to their at-risk business models, bad actors taking advantage of unforeseeable flaws in the systems, unintended (both "bad" and "good") consequences, naysayers/Pollyannas, confused/enlightened legislators/bureaucrats, and pundits, pundits, pundits, so too has the dis-intermediated sharing economy of other industries.

Of course, there's no going back either for music or for these other industries. Whether Uber, Lyft, or some new entrant claims dominance, we'll never go back to the old Taxi system any more than musicians will go back to a system that required them to trade the copyright in their sound recording (in perpetuity) in exchange for a label's funding of the recording, nor will customers go back to paying for downloads of albums when they can stream any song they like.

Internet of Things:

So, where is the Music Canary fluttering next? One fairly obvious use case of music leading the way to widespread adoption will be the aggressively sputtering Internet of Things movement.

I say "aggressively sputtering" not because I believe that IoT is in any way flailing, but because it currently lacks a "killer app" to pull it out of the early adopter/early majority channel in which it appears stuck.

I believe that the IoT killer app could be Amazon's Echo because of music.

I stated back in April that I thought the Echo was "one of Amazon's potentially more innovative products." If demand is any indicator (it is), the backordered status over Christmas of this device shows that others agree.

Having lived with the Echo since June, I can definitively state that it's the first IoT device that really integrates in a manner that goes beyond gimmicky, and that is easily utilized by people other than just nerds like me who spend an inordinate amount of time hacking together IFTTT recipes. **Dominantly, this is because of music.**

While you can utilize the Echo to get weather forecasts, the time, and—again, if you're a nerd—use it to voice control your lights, etc., its current magic lies in the fact that you can walk into the room and say, "Alexa, play Paul Desmond," and instantly the room fills with God's gift to the alto sax.

There's no unlocking of an iPhone and opening apps, and swiping and waiting. To use an Apple phrase, "it just works."

I am a deeply passionate, fervent Sonos fan, and by no means does the sound of the Echo compare to that of the Sonos system, but you know who doesn't care? My wife, my kids, and their friends, and also about 99% of the population who have neither the desire nor time to figure out how to open the Sonos app, wait for it to load—even a few seconds is too long, pick a music source, and pick a Sonos device to stream to when they can just walk into a room and say, "Alexa, play 'Good to Be Alive.'"

If IoT is to really integrate in a meaningful way—and I believe it will—it will be led by the approach that Echo has taken with music. That is, a dead-simple application that, while only hinting at the underlying potential of the device, delights the user enough to engage them in a manner that initiates usage and spurs further exploration.

My wife, for instance, now uses the Echo to not only call up music, but also to turn on and off the lights. Music was the leading edge—but for her being pulled into the Echo IoT world by music, she never would have engaged.

Virtual Reality:

No one doubts that VR is upon us, and that 2016 is likely to be the year when it becomes vastly more widespread. As my friend and colleague, Benji Rogers and I discussed in a conversation in two parts, we both believe that it will be music that largely drives the VR adoption.

Blockchain:

Through artists like Imogen Heap we're already seeing music push Blockchain technology into a larger public consciousness, and—as is often the case—other industries, from VR (see above) to fine art to finance, are watching/following/engaging.

So, predicting that Blockchain tech will be more prominent in 2016 isn't a very bold statement, but—again—the point of this piece is more to show that we should be watching the music space for clues as to where other industries will land, and right now music is pushing Blockchain, and vice versa.

Empathy:

I'll end this column—my last of 2015— with my own personal hope for 2016.

In a handful of columns this year, I've written the following:

"Now more than ever—with so much talk about building walls that not only (in theory) keep others out, but also ensnare those within— empathy is crucial. Empathy allows us to overcome our fear of the "other"; to expand the circles—whether they are of our own makings or created by political forces—to be more inclusive in nature.

Art, generally, and music, specifically, has long been a force for this type of empathic expansion. When we are emotionally moved by a piece of music, the arbitrary "otherness"—whether based on differences of skin color or religious/sexual orientation—begins to fall away, and understanding of commonality ensues. In short: More Art Equals Less War."

I truly hope and believe that it will be music and art that will cut through the divisive rhetoric and fear, and lead to understanding and empathy. This is truly the purpose of music, and it's what keeps us coming back to it—irrespective of the business elements surrounding it.

At its core, music isn't so much a canary in a coalmine, but rather a homing pigeon that somehow, someway knows how to help us find our way home.

HOW BLOCKCHAIN COULD HELP KANYE USE FACEBOOK TO GET OUT OF DEBT—AND SOLVE FACEBOOK'S VIDEO PROBLEM

Feb 15, 2016

In a series of tweets, Kanye West called on Mark Zuckerberg (and, in a seeming afterthought, Larry Page) to "help [him]" by investing "1 billion dollars into Kanye West."

On one hand, this request seems to come from financial imperative: "I write this to you my brothers while still 53 million dollars in personal debt... "

On the other, a sense that Mr. Zuckerberg, et al., should generally be doing more to support artists:

"All you dude in San Fran play rap music in your homes but never help the real artists…"

Hard to know exactly what's going on here—according to MarketWatch, Mr. West is worth an estimated $100 million. Far be it from me, however, to question someone's personal balance sheet or motives.

I do, however, have a suggestion that could speak to both of Mr. West's issues by using Blockchain Technology to increase his revenue from Mr. Zuckerberg's Facebook.

As most of us have encountered, uploading video to Facebook can be problematic if that video has copyrighted music in it.

There are a host of rights issues related to combining copyrighted music with video and then reproducing, distributing, and broadcasting (i.e. publicly performing) that video.

Absent the appropriate licenses between the rights holders of the music and the parties using the music, there is potentially copyright infringement. The risk of this infringement is what forces Facebook (and others) to put systems in place to attempt to block the posting of infringing material on their site.

The downside of this approach, however, is that not only are those attempting to post their videos frustrated/confused/disappointed, and, of course, the viewers of these music-less videos have a suboptimal experience, *but so too are artists, like Mr. West, potentially harmed by this approach.*

For instance, currently, if you shoot a video of your cat doing something adorable while Mr. West's music is playing in the background, and you then try to upload this video to Facebook, for the reasons iterated above, you will likely not be able to.

However, what if you were presented with the option to pay some small fee to post this cat/Kanye West video to Facebook? Would you pay a dollar for this right? A penny?

Certainly, many people would refuse to pay anything, but others would pay.

How many would pay? How much? Who knows.

Currently, there's no possible way to know if a market exists for people to pay for music used in this way. Just as before Facebook and Zynga created a market for people to pay for things like virtual livestock in Farmville, few people conceived of such a transaction.

Of course, rights and transactions around music are far

more complex than those around virtual livestock (I suppose), and that's where emergent technology such as Blockchain could provide a solution.

Here's how: utilizing Blockchain Technology, Mr. West would create a record of his work on the Bitcoin Blockchain and ascribe that work with data and rights that would delineate what uses and at what price he would approve.

By utilizing so-called "Smart Contracts"—that are a key element of Blockchain Technology—whenever someone attempted to use Mr. West's work in a way he delineated, the "contract" would execute, and the money would flow directly to Mr. West (or his designees), and the user would have the ability to use his work in the limited manner stipulated by the Smart Contract.

Put simply: Mr. West creates a set of rules; such as, "[Song X] may be synchronized to a video created by any individual (i.e. non-business), and posted to their personal Facebook page in consideration for [some amount of currency]."

Of course, the video would have to adhere to Facebook's general terms of service, which would reduce the risk of the song being synchronized with video that a reasonable person would find offensive.

Additional rules—via the Smart Contract—could be added as well: perhaps once the video is viewed, shared, Liked, etc. over a certain number of times, an additional payment would have to be made or the video would be removed.

Even with very small individual transaction amounts, such a solution could lead to material revenue—imagine the num-

ber of people who are currently frustrated by not being able to utilize Mr. West's and other's music in their Facebook videos.

Some artists, of course, will desire not to participate in such a system, and they should absolutely not be forced to do so. Other artists will embrace this with gusto, and perhaps encourage their fans (by offering their music at a lower rate) to utilize their music in their homemade videos.

Of course, an additional benefit is promotion. In this scenario, the artists' music would potentially be exposed to a host of people who could become fans...people who—absent such a Blockchain Technology solution—would potentially never hear the music.

Are there issues/problems/flaws/details to be worked through with this? Of course. Are they surmountable? Impossible to know, but—as a rule—when market demand meets technological innovation, solutions emerge. I would argue we have the market demand, and we're perilously close (if not already there) to having the sufficient technology.

FROM MODELING TO MEASURING: A BLOCKCHAIN SOLUTION FOR MUSIC AT POLITICAL EVENTS

Jul 27, 2016

Every election cycle since Reagan's 1984 campaign has included—to a greater or lesser degree—tension around the use of music by candidates during their events. In fact, while Reagan's misguided use of "Born in the USA" was the first truly memorable and visible kerfuffle, it's likely that, to paraphrase Raymond Kurzweil, it's not that the (mis)-usage of music is getting worse, but that our information with respect to reporting it has gotten better.

In any case, here we are again, and nary a day goes by when there aren't pleas/demands from artists for politicians to stop using their music, and the media seems to be more engaged than ever in reporting this phenomenon. Yours truly was even recently on NECN discussing Donald Trump's use of music during the RNC, and—at only a slightly more visible level [wink]—John Oliver devoted a large portion of his weekly show to the subject, and even created a song—featuring artists like Josh Groban, Usher, Sheryl Crowe, and others—that articulated these artists' frustrations around the issue (I've written about how problematic this song is in terms of the artists' seeming misunderstanding of the rights issues, entitled, "Do Artists Like Usher And Josh Groban Really Not Know How They Make Their Money?").

With respect to whether or not politicians can use artists' music: briefly, if these artists are the songwriters and have affiliated with a Performance Rights Organization (PRO), like ASCAP, SESAC, or BMI, and the venues in which these events are taking place have purchased a blanket license to publicly perform the songs that are in the catalogs of these organizations, these candidates are within their rights to do so.

While in most other countries creators of works can rely on "Moral Rights," the United States does not recognize this concept. This concept of Moral Rights is succinctly summed up by Betsy Rosenblatt from Harvard Law School:

"...the ability of authors to control the eventual fate of their works. An author is said to have the "moral right" to control her work. The concept of moral rights thus relies on the connection between an author and her creation. Moral rights protect the personal and reputational, rather than purely monetary, value of a work to its creator."

While authors in the US can conceivably rely on claims such as False Endorsement to stop those who are using their works against their wishes, this approach is time-consuming and costly, and certainly victory is not guaranteed.

Thus, there is currently no practical legal mechanism for artists to avail themselves of in order to stop the unwanted use of their work. The problem, however, is less a legal one, and more a systems problem.

The reason, for instance, that Queen doesn't just withdraw their music from the PRO with whom they are affiliated, and thereby force candidates and/or venues to directly license their work, is because this would also preclude them from collecting the massive amounts of money their songs generate via usages that one assumes they are OK with.

Undoubtedly, the Quicken Loans Arena in Cleveland, where the RNC Convention took place, has blanket licenses with the PROs in place. And, certainly at some point after the RNC Convention ended, some other event took place in this arena—perhaps a sporting event—during which songs like "We Are the Champions" and/or "We Will Rock You" were played (because one or both of those songs are always played at a sporting event), and the members of Queen who wrote those songs would eventually receive compensation for the public performance of those songs via a percentage of the blanket license fees collected and distributed by their PRO (this, of course, also means they will eventually receive payment for Trump's usage).

This issue—Queen and most other artists being stuck in a dynamic where they cannot feasibly select where, when, and how their music is publicly performed—highlights how we must aggressively move from a system of "modeling" to one of "measuring." This "from modeling to measuring" phrase was coined by my brilliant friend, Kelly Olson, from Intel, and it succinctly sums up the problem [disclosure, Intel is a client of my consulting firm].

Think of it this way: for decades (and for many still today), your electricity usage was "modeled." That is, very occasionally, the energy company would send a representative out to take a meter reading, and, based on these periodic readings, the energy company would model (estimate) a bill for the other months when they didn't (because it wasn't technologically/economically practical to do so) take actual readings (i.e. measure).

As technology advanced, of course, energy companies have been able to move from a modeling approach of approximation to a measuring approach of knowing precisely how much energy you are using.

Certainly, music being played at arenas—particularly prerecorded music—could easily be measured, rather than still being modeled. For example, a Shazam-like listening device could be deployed to capture which songs are being played in real time.

In this manner, artists would know precisely when and in what context their music is being used. This would not only allow for artists to have better information, but for venues too to be able to have a better sense of the precise cost related to their music use.

In other words, currently venues must pay a blanket license fee that allows them to publicly perform *anything* in the PROs' catalogs. Of course, they play only a fraction of the songs in the catalog, even though they're paying for the right to play everything. But if, instead, they could simply choose the precise songs they want to play, they could do a cost/benefit analysis and pay for the songs they perceive as creating value, and not pay for the ones they don't desire to use.

The artists could add conditions. For example, they might refuse to allow to have their music publicly performed during

political events; and, via this measuring approach, the artists would know if these explicit conditions had been violated and be able to take legal action and/or raise their prices to address these unwanted usages.

Of course, there are issues with this approach. Dominantly, that while this modeling approach appears to be technologically feasible for recorded music at venues, this type of usage is only a fraction of the total usages—music in restaurants, small clubs, live music, generally, etc.— that require licenses. Certainly, blanket licenses (i.e. the modeling approach) were, and still may be, the most efficient way to address these types of usages.

However, as technology continues to advance, the ability to measure rather than model will become more pervasive, and even music performed live in small clubs will be able to be accurately tracked.

In this manner, actual free markets—rather than "markets" governed by Consent Decrees—could emerge.

Would such a measuring model obviate the PROs? Perhaps. I suggested as much over a year ago in an article in this space entitled, "Bitcoin Can't Save The Music Industry Because the Music Industry Will Resist Transparency." But, perhaps not. The PROs—like any other firm—must innovate or die. Certainly, they could play the dominant role in leading this change, and, in so doing, secure their places going forward via adding value.

With respect to specifics around how **Blockchain Technology** would come into play, there are several reasons why this tech would facilitate this measuring approach in a superior way to a simple database solution:

First, the distributed nature of Blockchains would ensure that the data is immutable, and therefore difficult to be altered/co-opted.

Second, the potential for a more transparent record of the usages would allow for both those using music and those whose music is being used to not only know with some degree of precision the types of usage, but—through this knowledge—to more efficiently price the usages and provide evidence in the case of disputes.

Third, via the "smart contract" functionality related to Blockchain Tech, a set of rules and requirements could be created by both those who desire their music to be used and those who desire to use music, and—when these requirements are met—transactions could occur in real time with more efficiency.

Fourth, new value could be created around the use of music, in particular with respect to those currently left out of the equation: performers. Currently, if a song is publicly performed, for instance in a venue, only the writer is compensated—the performer of the song is not (when Whitney Houston's version of Dolly Parton's composition "I Will Always Love You" is played at a stadium, Dolly Parton is paid, Whitney Houston's estate is not). Rights holders could require—via contract—that both performers and writers be compensated.

Fifth, dynamic pricing could emerge. As an example of going from modeling to measuring, think of how Uber dynamically raises their prices (the dreaded "surge pricing") via measuring when demand exceeds supply, while the taxi industry dominantly uses a modeling approach, and does not dynamically alter their pricing. Music could do the same.

We're moving from a society that models to one that measures. We see data going from unstructured to structured in everything from wearable health to sleep to productivity; soon we'll quantify virtually everything in our lives in order to optimize our usages. Music will—sooner or later—move to this measuring approach as well, and—at that point—musicians will have vastly more degrees of not only control of how/when their music is used, but also how to monetize these usages.

HATERS GONNA HATE: WHY THOSE CELEBRATING THE "DEATH" OF THE BITCOIN BLOCKCHAIN ARE MISSING THE POINT

Jan 23, 2016

Mike Hearn, one of the original members of the Bitcoin development team, recently stated that the "Bitcoin experiment" has failed:

> "Why has Bitcoin failed? It has failed because the community has failed. What was meant to be a new, decentralized form of money that lacked "systemically important institutions" and "too big to fail" has become something even worse: a system completely controlled by just a handful of people. Worse still, the network is on the brink of technical collapse. The mechanisms that should have prevented this outcome have broken down, and as a result there's no longer much reason to think Bitcoin can actually be better than the existing financial system."

In the short period of time since Mr. Hearn wrote his post, it's been interesting to watch the response. Certain people seem to revel in some strange form of "told ya so" schadenfreude, while others are ignoring/dismissing Mr. Hearn's proclamation.

I will never understand the mindset of a person who

would actively root against a technology with such great potential —unless, of course, that person benefits from the current state of technology, as I discussed in an article entitled: "Bitcoin Can't Save The Music Industry Because the Music Industry Will Resist Transparency."

I also am skeptical of people who blithely disregard the challenges facing any new technological advancement, and who make light of the difficulties of crossing the chasm from early adopters to a more mainstream adoption.

So, is the Bitcoin Blockchain over? Is it now in an inexorable slow-moving death spiral towards obsolescence?

I don't know. Could be. Might not be.

Of course, no one else knows with any degree of certainty either, but I (and others) put a lot of stock in what the Venture Capitalist Fred Wilson thinks about emergent technologies, and he had this to say about Mr. Hearn's post:

> "The Bitcoin experiment is six years old. There has been a significant amount of venture capital investment in the Bitcoin ecosystem. There are a number of well-funded companies competing to build valuable businesses on top of this technology. We are invested in at least one of them. And the competition between these various companies and their visions has played a part in the stalemate. These companies have a lot to gain or lose if Bitcoin survives or fails. So, I expect that there will be some rationality, brought on by cap-

> italist behavior, that will emerge or maybe is already emerging."

But, for a moment, let's step back from the prognostication, and instead imagine that, yes (to the odd delight of some people), the Bitcoin Blockchain has failed. It's over.

Where would that leave us?

Anyone who has spent any time in the tech or startup world knows and understands that success and adoption is an iterative process.

While the Apple Newton and the Rio PMP300 mp3 player were "failures," the technologies related to their development and launch (and, yes, failure) endured and were instrumental in terms of the development of future successful products.

Some of the most enduring posts I've written speak to this type of creeping, iterative development that largely goes unnoticed by the masses - until these same masses wake up one day to a deeply changed world:

"The Stream that Snuck up on You"

About how streaming music and video services "suddenly" became prevalent in peoples' lives.

"The Cloud That Snuck up on You"

About how cloud services "suddenly" became prevalent in peoples' lives.

I'm currently working on similar articles on technologies that are following this same trajectory:

> "The Internet of Things that Snuck up on You"
> "The Artificial Intelligence that Snuck up on You"

The above articles will, of course, address the fact that both IoT and AI are already here and upon us; that they—via a long, iterative process—have crossed the chasm from early adopter land to early majority, and will soon be squarely in the middle/majority of the distribution curve.

The Bitcoin Blockchain—success or failure—has similarly established a durable beachhead upon which technology will continue to build upon.

In other words, in the larger scheme of things, it doesn't really matter if the Bitcoin Blockchain "fails," because it has already attained a sense of permanence to the degree that it's inconceivable that other technologies will not be built upon its principles and technologies. And, perhaps, more importantly, the ethos of Bitcoin Blockchain—transparency and disintermediation—will similarly endure and be built upon.

And so, even if the Bitcoin Blockchain does "fail," some variant of the Bitcoin Blockchain will not be a failure.

Specifically, the Bitcoin Blockchain has either more widely established or completely originated certain core technological and conceptual components, such as:

- Decentralized Registries
- Smart Contracts
- Transparent (or not, users decide) and Immutable Records of creation/creators
- Transparent records of transactions
- Disintermediated Payments
- Payments with little-to-no transaction costs
- The Mining system of incentive
- Proof of Work/Hash systems
- Incented sharing (as illustrated by Imogen Heap's Mycelia)

Does any rational person think that any/all of these things are going to —poof—disappear and retreat to some troglodytic cave? Suggesting such a thing is no more reasonable than asserting that CDs will make a comeback.

And guess what, ***some*** of us ***knew*** that CDs were done the moment we laid eyes on the Rio MP3 player ("failure" that it was). I'll never forget that moment; ***I was running a record label at the time.***

So...sure, the Bitcoin Blockchain may very well go the way of the Rio, but be very clear, the technological innovations and the general shift in mindset that have been developed and occurred because of the Bitcoin Blockchain cannot and will not ever die. In fact, it's just getting started. Ignore at your peril.

Made in the USA
Monee, IL
17 April 2021

ABOUT THE AUTHO

From a leading thinker, writer, educator, and entrepreneur in space, *Everything In Its Right Place* is a natural byproduc George Howard's ongoing work in Blockchain Tech.

Mr. Howard's career has been defined by a passionate driv leverage technology in order to create dramatic value. Mr. Hov has consistently demonstrated a keen ability to not only discern technologies that represent opportunity, but to also implen them in a manner that maximizes impact and ROI.

An artist by nature, a JD/MBA by training, and an entre neur, academic, and operator in practice, Mr. Howard has sta run, and advised some of the largest and most significant cor nies in the world, from running the first CD-only label, to dri disintermediation in the distribution industry via co-founding of the world's largest independent distributors, to defining and plementing the then-nascent Social Media technology for For 500 companies and Ivy League Universities.

All of the above is a byproduct of his personal mission: artists create sustainable careers on their own terms. He is gu by the deeply-rooted belief that art is an empathy machine, thus, more art equals less war.